SO-BDH-320

BILLY GRAHAM

Evangelistic Association

Always Good News.

Dear Friend,

I am pleased to send you this copy of *Defying Normal* by Skip Heitzig, pastor at Calvary Albuquerque in New Mexico and host of *The Connection*. He has spoken at the Billy Graham Training Center at The Cove and is a good friend to me and to this ministry.

Our nation's moral landscape has changed drastically in recent years, and it's easy for believers to feel like strangers in their own country. But we're not called to conform—God wants us to shine His light in the darkness. In *Defying Normal*, Skip challenges us to remain obedient to God's Word and offers practical strategies for exercising self-control, living out our faith, and acting with humility, despite pressure from a hostile culture. I pray that this book inspires you to stand boldly for Jesus, *"the author and finisher of our faith"* (Hebrews 12:2, NKJV).

For more than 65 years, the Billy Graham Evangelistic Association has worked to take the Good News of Jesus Christ throughout the world by every effective means available, and I'm excited about what God will do in the years ahead.

We would appreciate knowing how our ministry has touched your life. May God richly bless you.

Sincerely,

Franklin Graham
President

If you would like to know more about our ministry, please contact us:

IN THE U.S.:
Billy Graham Evangelistic Association
1 Billy Graham Parkway
Charlotte, NC 28201-0001
BillyGraham.org
info@bgea.org
Toll-free: 1-877-247-2426

IN CANADA:
Billy Graham Evangelistic
Association of Canada
20 Hopewell Way NE
Calgary, AB T3J 5H5
BillyGraham.ca
Toll-free: 1-888-393-0003

Praise for *Defying Normal*

My friend pastor Skip Heitzig has penned a book for our times. As he always does from Scripture, Skip teaches the importance of bowing before the King of Heaven. In doing so, we are strengthened to live boldly while standing in the midst of an unbelieving world. Brace yourself when you read *Defying Normal*, because you will find yourself *Soaring above the Status Quo!*

Franklin Graham, President and CEO, Samaritan's Purse
Billy Graham Evangelistic Association

If you long to see God use your life and break free from just flipping pages on the calendar—learn from a proven leader and contagious Christian like Skip Heitzig. Follow his example in *Defying Normal* and soon you'll be soaring too.

Dr. James MacDonald, Senior Pastor, Harvest Bible Chapel, Chicago

In this book Skip helps us grasp the biblical concept that God never intended for us to settle for "normal"; He grants us the grace and strength to withstand the suffocating intrusion of unjust laws and cultural pressures. Say good-bye to "normal" and be reminded that God walks with His people even when the path becomes difficult!

Dr. Erwin W. Lutzer, Senior Pastor, The Moody Church, Chicago

Fitting in is easy in our everything-goes culture, but it takes a certain kind of bravery to stand against the status quo and be different. In *Defying Normal*, Skip gives us the courage to look normal in the face and defy it. This is my kind of book.

Kristen Welch, Author of the blog *We are THAT family*
and founder of Mercy House

In a time when followers of Jesus Christ face more opposition to their beliefs than previous generations, Skip challenges us to stand boldly, act wisely, and to live faithfully in a hostile cultural and political environment. *Defying Normal: Soaring Above the Status Quo* will call you to courageous and convictional faith and equip you to effectively share your beliefs in a way that glorifies God.

Dr. Jack Graham, Pastor, Prestonwood Baptist Church, Plano, TX

In his new book my friend and godfather pastor Skip Heitzig will teach you how to live the wild, free life 30,000 feet above the status quo that you were born to live. Normal is overrated, and the adventure that is your calling is waiting—there's not a moment to lose!

Levi Lusko, Pastor, Fresh Life Church, Montana
Author of *Through the Eyes of a Lion*

Pastor Skip does a wonderful job at taking an ancient narrative and making it feel part of everyday living. More importantly, he takes principles and turns them into practical application while revealing the heart, nature, and integrity of Daniel while he defies normal.

Bianca Juarez Olthoff, Chief Storyteller for The A21 Campaign

Defying Normal is a clarion call to extraordinary living. Using the story of Daniel, Skip calls Christians to embrace a radical life of faith, humility, integrity, courage, and more. If you read this book and take its principles to heart, you just might be surprised how God may use you.

Dr. Sean McDowell, Author of *A New Kind of Apologist*

DEFYING N0RMAL

SOARING ABOVE
THE STATUS QUO

SKIP HEITZIG
WITH JEFF KINLEY

WORTHY®
PUBLISHING

This *Billy Graham Library Selection* special edition is published with
permission from Worthy Publishing Group.

A *Billy Graham Library Selection* designates materials that are appropriate for a well-rounded collection of quality Christian literature, including both classic and contemporary reading and reference materials.

This *Billy Graham Library Selection* special edition is published with permission from Worthy Publishing Group.

©2015 by Skip Heitzig

Published by Worthy Books, an imprint of Worthy Publishing Group, a division of Worthy Media, Inc., One Franklin Park, 6100 Tower Circle, Suite 210, Franklin, TN 37067.

WORTHY is a registered trademark of Worthy Media, Inc.

HELPING PEOPLE EXPERIENCE THE HEART OF GOD

eBook available wherever digital books are sold.

Library of Congress Control Number: 2015947984

All rights reserved. No portion of this book may be reproduced, stored in a retrieval system, or transmitted in any form or by any means—electronic, mechanical, photocopy, recording, scanning, or other—except for brief quotations in critical reviews or articles, without the prior written permission of the publisher.

Unless otherwise noted, Scripture quotations are taken from the New King James Version®. ©1982 by Thomas Nelson. Used by permission. All rights reserved.

Scripture quotations marked NLT are taken from the Holy Bible, New Living Translation, ©1996, 2004, 2007 by Tyndale House Foundation. Used by permission of Tyndale House Publishers, Inc., Carol Stream, IL 60188. All rights reserved. Scripture quotation marked ESV is taken from the ESV® Bible (The Holy Bible, English Standard Version®) ©2001 by Crossway, a publishing ministry of Good News Publishers. ESV® Text Edition: 2011. The ESV® text has been reproduced in cooperation with and by permission of Good News Publishers. Unauthorized reproduction of this publication is prohibited. All rights reserved. Scripture quotation taken from the NEW AMERICAN STANDARD BIBLE®, ©1960, 1962, 1963, 1968, 1971, 1972, 1973, 1975, 1977, 1995 by The Lockman Foundation. Used by permission. Scripture quotation marked NIV is taken from THE HOLY BIBLE, NEW INTERNATIONAL VERSION®, NIV® ©1973, 1978, 1984, 2011 by Biblica, Inc.® Used by permission. All rights reserved worldwide.

Italics added to direct Scripture quotations are the author's emphasis.

For foreign and subsidiary rights, contact rights@worthypublishing.com

Published in association with William K. Jensen Literary Agency, www.wkjacency.com

ISBN: 978-1-59328-552-4 (BGEA edition)
Previous ISBN: 978-1-61795-608-9

Cover Design: Bill Chiaravalle / BrandNavigation
Interior Design and Typesetting: Bart Dawson

Printed in the United States of America

To my grandchildren, Seth Nathaniel and Kaydence Joy,
who are bright spots in my world.
It is my hope that they will follow the example of Daniel
in their generation and defy normal.
May they show others how to rise above the status quo
that will permeate their world.

C^ONTENTS

NOTE FROM AN UNAPOLOGETIC NONCONFORMIST

I hate the status quo. As far back as I can remember I have bucked against it, as conforming is not my strong suit. Of course, I realize that being a nonconformist can be a character flaw, but I have many friends and colleagues who fit into the same category. We've learned that going against the status quo can sometimes bring great results.

Years ago, when there was an embargo on supplies going into Iraq after the first Gulf War, I defied the status quo and traveled into Baghdad with a courageous team to bring gifts wrapped in shoeboxes to distribute to children. The result was a statement made on Iraqi public television that Jesus loves *all* the children of the world! The earliest apostles defied the status quo in Jerusalem when they brought the gospel to that city, even though a mandatory silence was imposed. William Wilberforce defied the status quo in England when he fought to abolish slavery amid cries to the contrary.

Henry David Thoreau observed that "the mass of men lead lives of quiet desperation."[1] I would amend his statement by adding that those who lead lives of quiet desperation are those who are afraid to upset the status quo.

Let's pause to consider what *status quo* really means. The phrase is of Latin origin and literally means "the state" (*status*) "in which" (*quo*), or the current state of affairs or the existing state of things.[2] That sounds okay—even admirable, right? But over time, the term has come to refer to things that are unchanged, indistinct, unimaginative, even boring. So when I say I hate the status quo, I'm referring to monotonous, repetitive, and boring lifestyles that lack divine purpose. Distasteful to me are the tedious activities by which people make a living yet lack real life! *Status quo is life without significance.* I bet you feel the same way.

Many people uphold the status quo because they want to fit in with the crowd. They relish the camaraderie of conformity. Deep inside we all want to stand out as individuals . . . just not too much. And we end up surrendering to "normal." This tendency starts at an early age because everyone wants to be liked. We feel pressured to conform to whatever is cool, hip, trendy, and stylish. We conform to fit in with the popular folks: the thin ones, the fashionable ones, the smart ones. That's because peer pressure is *real* pressure.

Status quo is life without significance.

One of my earliest memories of wanting to fit in was during my teenage years. I wanted a car like all the cool kids in school, but my dad was convinced I should save up and buy a car with my own money. Fortunately for me, my brother had a '67 Plymouth for sale. Unfortunately, it was a car most junkyards would have turned away! However, to me, having some wheels was better than no wheels, and I persuaded him to sell it to me for about forty dollars. My car didn't have a muffler, wouldn't engage in second gear, and was in dire need of a paint job. Its Bondo gray primer skin screamed individuality—just not the kind I particularly wanted as a high schooler. Finally, I fit in because I had a car. But sadly, I stood out too much because my car was so old and loud that you could hear it coming from a mile away. There were times I wished I had no car rather than my car. And that taught me an important lesson: fitting in isn't always what it's cracked up to be.

There comes a time when we must decide that individuality for the right reason is better than conformity for the wrong reason. We all wish we could be ourselves and want the crowd to look up to us. But that rarely happens. The tug of the status quo in our world is too strong. So that leads us to asking some serious questions, like:

Who am I going to be?

Who am I going to please?

Exactly whose standard am I going to conform to?

In the 1960s, they called this being "countercultural." But did you know that the Bible actually encourages us be countercultural? Paul said, "Do not be conformed to this world, but be transformed by the renewing of your mind" (Romans 12:2). By "transformed" he meant utterly, totally changed. Call it an extreme makeover. That is the intent of *Defying Normal:*

Soaring Above the Status Quo—to help you change your life. You don't have to lead a life of quiet desperation. You don't have to go along and live the mundane or blend in with those who fly under the radar. You can defy what is popularly accepted as normal and rise above the boring crowd!

Defying Normal revolves around underlying principles from the life of Daniel, an amazing person in the Old Testament. Daniel stands out as a courageous nonconformist whose life made a difference in his time. He endures as a role model today for people who dare to be countercultural, who are willing to stand out from the crowd and soar above their circumstances. Facing a hostile political structure that didn't square with his own convictions, Daniel confronted jealous colleagues who conspired against him in order to shut him up. He tackled the challenge of living as a refugee in a foreign land while striking the balance between gracious compliance and brazen nonconformity.

When you think about it, Daniel was a lot like Jesus—a balance between gracious compliance to God and brazen nonconformity to the world.

MY STORY OF DEFYING NORMAL

On a more personal level, let me briefly tell you my story of defying normal—my challenge to my religious upbringing.

I'm not a religious person. People who know me as a pastor are sometimes astonished when I say this. Often people who see me in public will say, "Oh, you're that preacher over at that church, aren't you? You're a religious person." But I'm not religious, and I'll point that out.

"Oh," they may continue, "I thought you were religious. You're a pastor, aren't you?"

"Yes, I'm a pastor," I admit, "but I'm not religious."

"How so?" they sometimes ask. I explain that religion is all about a system of organized rituals, beliefs, and traditions. Christianity may include some of these elements, but it is much more than a system; it's all about a relationship with the living God through Jesus Christ. Christianity is not about rituals or a system; it's about the relationship a person has with Jesus Christ. I never found Jesus in religion. True, I grew up religious. And in the system I grew up in, there was talk about Jesus. They even sang songs about Jesus and sort of religiously tipped their hats to Jesus here and there. But there's a difference between the ritual of a religious life and the reality of a redeemed life.

> There's a difference between the ritual of a religious life and the reality of a redeemed life.

The most significant event of my entire life occurred when I was eighteen years of age. That summer, shortly after my birthday, I was converted and authentically gave my life to Jesus Christ. After months of wrestling with plans for my future and trying to figure out what life was all about, I came to a point of decision—I resolved to make Jesus Christ my chief pursuit.

Through a simple prayer, I placed my trust in Christ as Savior. From that day onward He has occupied the foremost place of honor and leadership in my life. The commitment to turn away from wrongful behavior and follow Jesus was the step of faith I needed. That decision made all the difference. Talk about defying normal!

Some people I had grown up with in my church took note of this. Most thought I was experiencing some sort of crisis and avoided me altogether. Others were curious to know more and asked me to appear before the leadership council of the church I had grown up in. They were curious to know my thoughts about why so many young people were leaving the church and what they needed to do about it. They asked me, "What do you think our church needs?" Now keep in mind, I was eighteen years old. I didn't have a lot of tact at that age.

So I bluntly replied, "This church needs Jesus Christ—crucified, risen from the dead, and personally living in your hearts."

That response did not go over as well as I thought it would. The church leaders felt a bit snubbed by a teenager lecturing them about the things of God, and my unmitigated zeal probably didn't help. Who did I think I was to stand in front of veteran clergy members and tell them how to get right with God? But I found myself doing just that. Some asked questions. Most just scowled.

My dad was in the crowd that day, and it didn't go over

well at home either. He let me know that my comments to the church leaders were disrespectful and unenlightened. He wanted to make sure I realized that nonconformity had its limits. Still, the fact remains that Jesus Christ is not religious and doesn't really care a whole lot for religion. He constantly butted heads with the establishment religion of His generation, challenging them, even rebuking many for hiding behind their rituals and sacraments.

So, even when I was eighteen, I felt that God wanted me to stand against the status quo of my day, to *defy normal*—the way things were in my family, church, and community.

Now, I'm not saying I even come close to what Daniel had to endure. But in my own way I understand what it means to kick against the normal expectations of living in a particular system.

RELIGION VERSUS RELATIONSHIP

You may be asking, "Let me get this straight: I *don't* have to join a religion in order to defy the world's expectations?" The answer to this question is yes and no. Yes, you should defy the world's expectations—but, no, you don't have to join a religion. Rather, you need to turn from sin and surrender to God, yearning for a personal relationship with a perfect Savior.

You may further wonder, "Is there really that big a difference between religion that acknowledges God and a relationship with God?"

Yes, I think there is.

First of all, I've discovered that religion is all about outward behavior, while Jesus focuses on the heart. Religion focuses on the outside, while Christ changes us from the inside out. Jesus called us to defy the normal standards of religion.

Second, religion is typically about the negatives. Jesus is all about freedom in the positives. Religion is filled with *you can't, you shouldn't, don't*, and a whole lot of *thou shalt nots*. But Jesus says, "Just come to Me, and I'll help you."

Third, religion sets up barriers you have to jump over to get to God. Jesus is all about knocking down barriers and making it possible for anyone to get to God. It's a huge difference.

I read a statement by Karl Marx years ago that really struck me. He said that religion "is the opium of the people."[3] I agree. Religion is an effective drug that controls people and the status quo. It numbs the minds of the masses, making them "normal."

Jesus doesn't do that.

Jesus defied normal. And what is true for Jesus was also true for Daniel.

DANIEL: A MAN WHO DEFIED NORMAL

In the person of Daniel the prophet, we meet a man much like Jesus. And as we'll see, God gave Daniel some big dreams. He defied the normal expectations with grace and ease through amazingly difficult circumstances.

The odds seemed stacked against him. As a young man living

in Jerusalem, Daniel was taken captive by the Babylonians and shuttled more than five hundred miles from his boyhood home. Throughout his life he faced despair, discouragement, derision, and even attempted death in this hostile foreign land. Yet he always triumphed above his circumstances . . . even into old age. And how did he do it? That is what you're about to discover.

Daniel was able to defy the "normal" of his day, surviving situations that would paralyze most people in fear. Instead of acting like a thermometer to reflect the ambient temperature of the surrounding world, he was more like a thermostat that changed the lives of the people he encountered. And even more astonishing, he left a legacy that continues to change people's lives today.

Daniel embodied eight elements that allowed him to soar above the status quo: self-control, faith, humility, integrity, dependence, courage, hope, and balance. These traits were not highly valued by the Babylonian empire he found himself in. And let's face it: these eight traits are not highly regarded in our society today. A few of them are respected but only when narrowly defined in a way that leaves God mostly out of the picture. But these eight character qualities set Daniel above the rest.

PRACTICAL WAYS TO DEFY NORMAL

One more thing before we get started. It's a great idea to spend time reading about Daniel's life and thinking about what it means for you, but it means nothing unless you find ways to apply it. That's why I've included a section at the end of each chapter called "Dare to Defy Normal."

I want you to challenge yourself to apply the concepts you learn in real, practical ways. Each section includes two kinds of prompts. The first is an invitation to *deliberate* on a point related to the chapter. Do some serious thinking and praying about it. The second prompt is an opportunity to *defy normal* and make an application in your life.

So when I say "I dare you" to do something, try not to think of it as me being pushy or obnoxious—you know, like *I double-dog dare you to defy normal*, with the implication being you're a spiritual wimp if you don't. Rather, I want to encourage you to build the kind of character that Daniel showed in his life—character that honored God and was, in turn, honored by God in challenging and tumultuous times. Of course, if you want to take it as a double-dog dare because it fires you up to defy normal and live for Christ, then I can live with that.

I don't know what circumstances you face, but I'm guessing that they include things like debt, despair, rejection, ill health, or possibly even death of your loved ones. But I do know that with God's help and with His time-tested truths, you can survive and thrive right where you are. I want to lift your eyes higher than the horizon you may be staring at and encourage you to dream bigger.

Are you ready to rise above the status quo and defy normal? If so, then let's go!

CHAPTER ONE

CONQUER Y0UR INNER SPACE

SELF-CONTROL

It was July 20, 1969, only a few days away from my fourteenth birthday. But I wasn't thinking about my age that day. Instead, my mind was miles away—237,680 miles, to be exact. Along with most of the world, I was glued to our rabbit-eared television as we watched astronaut Neil Armstrong open the hatch of the Apollo 11 Lunar Module *Eagle* and descend to the moon's surface. The spectral black-and-white images were beamed back to my family and at least six hundred million other people on earth. It seemed the entire planet collectively held its breath as Armstrong took his first step on the moon. *We really did it!* I thought. *Our astronaut just walked on the moon!*

As a young teenager, I felt like we could conquer anything

now. And that boyish sensation of invincibility was further fed by Armstrong's famous words, "That's one small step for a man, one giant leap for mankind."[1] Another member of the *Apollo 11* mission, Buzz Aldrin, joined him. He described the view of the moon as "magnificent desolation."[2] After years of competing with Russia, the United States had finally conquered outer space.

However, while such a conquest was an epic and historical achievement, I believe there is a greater, more rewarding challenge—conquering *inner* space. The moonscape might have been a desolate place to Buzz Aldrin, but the inner workings of the human heart can be even more barren. The prophet Jeremiah described the bleakness of our condition as "deceitful above all things, and desperately wicked" (Jeremiah 17:9). Conquering humankind's inner space is an even more noble pursuit than dominating the vast expanse of our galaxies. The battles we face against anger, doubt, insecurity, lust, jealousy, envy, suspicion, greed, and desire demand the very best of our capabilities. Why? Because the gravity pulling us downward toward earthly tendencies is strong. And defying this downward tug will take everything you've got.

A LIFELONG PURSUIT

Conquering our inner space is a lifelong pursuit, though I've met some people who think they've already arrived—and trust me, they're no fun to deal with. M. R. DeHaan, an accomplished physician and Bible teacher, said, "Self-satisfaction is the death of progress. . . . The most boring people I ever meet are the ones who take up my time telling me what they have done, when they ought to be doing more."[3]

Let's face it: we won't *arrive* until we reach heaven. In fact, we should never be satisfied with where we are. The apostle Paul wasn't content with his spiritual achievements. He said, "Not that I have already attained, or am already perfected; but I press on" (Philippians 3:12). The desire to overcome our limitations and imperfections is what compels us upward and moves us onward. In biblical terms, we long to overcome "the sin which so easily ensnares us" (Hebrews 12:1). But we can only do this with supernatural help. Only a divine enabling is sufficient for our divine calling.

Have you ever wondered how an airplane sitting on the tarmac could possibly get off the ground? Aeronautics teaches that the law of gravity, though formidable, can be superseded by thrust and lift. A Boeing 777 weighs as much as 775,000 pounds and can carry up to 550 passengers.[4] But how can an object of such size and weight be anything but earthbound? How can it possibly overcome the force of gravity? It's done by going fast enough and applying Newton's third law of motion. That law ensures that the air passing over the upward tilting wings will gain speed and be redirected downward. Engineers designed the

> Only a divine enabling is sufficient for our divine calling.

craft by applying mathematical aerodynamics to calculate lift and thrust so that even the heaviest objects can defy gravity. That still amazes me.

For believers, the only way to rise above the drag of sinful life on earth is to rely on a greater power—*God's* power. When we apply divine dynamics to our lives, "things which are impossible with men are possible with God" (Luke 18:27). Only God can supply the needed thrust to lift us above our earthbound human nature.

COUNT ON THE UNEXPECTED

A once-popular bumper sticker read, "Life happens." However, if it were up to me, I'd rephrase it to say, "Life happens *unexpectedly.*" You know what I'm talking about, don't you? You're going along your merry way when—*boom!*—Everything changes. Nations experience it. Businesses experience it. Families and individuals experience it. Maybe you faced the unexpected when your spouse asked for a divorce. Or when you answered a phone call in the middle of the night informing you that your son or daughter had been in a terrible accident. Or when the doctor delivered bad news after your blood work confirmed cancer. Suddenly, your life felt out of control.

I know because I've been there. I will never forget the night my dad phoned me to say my brother had been killed in a motorcycle crash. I was in my early twenties when my brother Bob died. He was closer in age to me than my other brothers, and losing him so suddenly was a defining moment for me. It was the first time I'd lost someone that close. I was jarred to the core. That tragic event introduced a level of uncertainty about the future I hadn't known until that moment. I had been with Bob only a few days earlier. But when life happened unexpectedly, I felt as if my life was spinning out of control.

Daniel had been there too.

DANIEL'S ENCOUNTER WITH THE UNEXPECTED

The unexpected happened for Daniel and the people of Jerusalem long ago. The Bible tells us,

> In the third year of the reign of Jehoiakim king of Judah, Nebuchadnezzar king of Babylon came to Jerusalem and besieged it. And the Lord gave Jehoiakim king of Judah into his hand, with some of the articles of the house of God, which he carried into the land of Shinar to the house of his god; and he brought the articles into the treasure house of his god. (Daniel 1:1–2)

Picture the scenario here. Life in Jerusalem was sweet. People were eating and drinking, waking and sleeping, buying and selling, laughing and crying, playing and working. Then one day they looked out the city gates and saw the Babylonian army surrounding them in attack mode. Suddenly, the Babylonians struck, killing many of Jerusalem's inhabitants. Those who survived were taken into captivity. And in a heartbeat, life turned from sweet to bitter.

The Bible gives us two statements that explain this event from different perspectives. The first describes the incident *historically*: "Nebuchadnezzar . . . came to Jerusalem and besieged it" (Daniel 1:1). History tells us that in the year 605 BC, young Nebuchadnezzar was a rising political star. He led the Babylonians in a decisive battle in Carchemish in southern Turkey. There, under Nebuchadnezzar, the Babylonians defeated two superpowers: Egypt and Assyria. After that, the rest of the world was free game for Babylonian rule. That same year, the Babylonians surrounded Jerusalem. They besieged Jerusalem two more times, in 597 BC and 586 BC, when they burned the Holy City. Today amid the archaeological ruins you can still see stones that bear the scorch marks of the fire set by the Babylonians. Jerusalem was blackened and bruised, and her people were hauled away to captivity.

This brings us to the second perspective—*God's*. Scripture says, "The Lord gave Jehoiakim king of Judah into his [Nebuchadnezzar's] hand" (Daniel 1:2). That's an extremely important statement. It seemed that Jerusalem was unexpectedly overtaken by Nebuchadnezzar, leaving the population either dead or taken captive. But the people shouldn't have been surprised. They had been warned this could happen. God told Moses, "The LORD will bring a nation against you from afar, from the end of the earth, as swift as the eagle flies, a nation whose language you will not understand, a nation of fierce countenance. . . . They shall besiege you at all your gates until your high and fortified walls, in which you trust, come down throughout all your land; and they shall besiege you at all your gates throughout all your land which the LORD your God has given you" (Deuteronomy 28:49–50, 52).

The Babylonian attack on Jerusalem seemed unexpected, but it was, in fact, predicted.

As time went on, prophets gave other warnings, each more precise, like this one from the prophet Isaiah: "Behold, the days are coming when all that is in your house, and what your fathers have accumulated until this day, shall be carried to Babylon; nothing shall be left," says the LORD. "And they shall take away some of your sons who will descend from you, whom you will beget; and they shall be eunuchs in the palace of the king of Babylon" (Isaiah 39:6–7). Could God have been any clearer? His prophet was 100 percent correct—and the Babylonians carried the Jews away to slavery.

From God's vantage point, this was all a divine setup. Nebuchadnezzar was the Babylonian bully who sang his own praises, playing other nations like strings on a harp. Little did he know that God was the orchestra director! In God's eyes, Nebuchadnezzar was merely a pawn on His chessboard to be moved around so that Daniel could attain a key position of influence.

When Jerusalem was overtaken and many were killed, Daniel

was one of those taken captive. Can you imagine seeing your young teenager taken captive to a country five hundred miles away? Then after abducting the kids, the Babylonians would kill their parents so the image of their parents' death would imprint in the minds of those children taken away in bondage.

But there are always two sides to history. The *factual* side tells us what happened: the how, what, when, and where. The *spiritual* side tells us why. In this case, Nebuchadnezzar attacked, and the Lord gave the people into his hands. These two perspectives were continually interwoven throughout Daniel's life— and yours. On one hand, man is active in history. On the other hand, God is active in history to bring about His purposes.

We can learn an important lesson from this. Life may happen unexpectedly, but God is working supernaturally. Rather than panic when things seem out of control, realize that God is at work behind the scenes.

Always.

I've heard it said, "God's ways are behind the scenes, but He moves all the scenes He is behind."

I can imagine those captives wondering, "How could a God of love let this happen? Why would God let the bad guys attack and win over the good guys?" But Daniel's perspective was more like Paul's when he was taken captive: "I want you to know, brethren, that the things which happened to me have actually turned out for the furtherance of the gospel" (Philippians 1:12).

Daniel would have agreed with Joseph, who said to his brothers who had sold him into captivity, "You meant evil against me; but God meant it for good" (Genesis 50:20).

Yes, life does happen unexpectedly . . . but God is active, even in the unexpected. My brother's unexpected death served as a wake-up call for me to rise above the status quo and be more deliberate about my life. After the grieving subsided, lessons about living with purpose and spiritual focus stayed with me. That horrible event served to change me for the better. What had previously been to me just a spiritual cliché—"all things work together for good to those who love God, to those who are the called according to His purpose" (Romans 8:28)—became a real-life principle.

> Life may happen unexpectedly, but God is working supernaturally.

A FOUR-PRONGED ATTEMPT TO CONFORM

To say that life in Babylon was challenging for Daniel would be an understatement. Though God had a plan, the world this young man found himself in didn't care anything for his God or for His plans. You know what that's like. Society expects you to conform to the status quo. The world is uncomfortable when you don't conform to its ideas and ways of doing things. In Babylon, Nebuchadnezzar used a well-formulated plan to take the cream-of-the-crop captives from the nations he conquered and train them to meet his "superior" standards. He established a four-pronged approach to compel his captives into his way of doing things.

First, he isolated them. Then he indoctrinated them. After this, he implemented the strategies of concession and confusion to bring the captives into line. But Daniel, when facing immense outward pressure, was able to stand firm because of the offsetting influence within him. Like a diver outfitted with a specially pressurized suit to counteract the force of the depth of the sea, God's people must be outfitted with pressurized dispositions so as not to be overcome by the force of the status quo.

The Babylonian conquerors could not conquer Daniel's buoyant soul. However, in order to conquer your own inner space, you'll need to understand the outside forces the enemy uses against you.

ISOLATION

Nebuchadnezzar took the best and brightest young men to Babylon, separating them from their family, their friends, *and* their faith. We're told he "instructed Ashpenaz, the master of his eunuchs, to bring some of the children of Israel and some of the king's descendants and some of the nobles, young men in whom there was no blemish, but good-looking, gifted in all wisdom, possessing knowledge and quick to understand, who had ability to serve in the king's palace" (Daniel 1:3–4). These young men were in a whole new world, totally isolated from familiar sights, sounds, and surroundings. The impressionable teenagers must have felt alone and confused so far from the land of their fathers and the ways of their people.

There are many factors today that can cause us to be isolated. For example, the Internet can make a person less comfortable with face-to-face interaction as he or she assumes a pseudonym online and derives empowerment from anonymous and unaccountable communication. Such social isolation often occurs when meaningful support is missing. A huge percentage of Americans don't have a single person they can confide in. Other factors like time spent in traffic commutes, longer working hours, and long periods of exposure to personalized media all take an isolating toll on the human psyche. Anything that moves us away from meaningful, real-life social ties and deep friendships pushes us further into social isolation. How many times have you seen a family at a restaurant together, each family member tuned out from the others while engaged on their phones?

INDOCTRINATION

Next, the young captives in Babylon were taught the "language and literature of the Chaldeans" (Daniel 1:4). You may wonder, *What's wrong with that? There's nothing immoral or sinful about learning another language.* However, their point was not merely to train the captives linguistically but to retrain them *philosophically.* Chaldean literature promoted an entirely different worldview. Imagine the impact the erudite Babylonian professors would make on young, impressionable Jewish minds. Everything the young captives had been taught would be challenged: their view of God, man, sin, and salvation. They would be expected to embrace a new, unbiblical worldview. Among other things, they were trained in the arts of divination, fortune-telling, astrology, reading omens, and the occult. These young Jewish men basically underwent a graduate-level course to make them forget everything they had learned growing up.

I recall my first day of college. The professor of my Integrated Zoology class felt it necessary to inform the entire classroom full of students that he would not tolerate a narrow, religious mindset in his class and that anyone who believed in God would be challenged. His stated aim was to undo such naiveté with a more refined and "intelligent" worldview. How many Christian college students have faced the same philosophical obstacles at secular university campuses? I find it interesting that teachers who are paid to teach English, chemistry, or biology often go out of their way to undermine the spiritual belief system of their students. I've talked with Christian college students who tell me they feel targeted as the secular system tries to dismantle their faith once they have left the shelter of their religious support system. Just as Daniel and his friends found, the world still works to isolate and indoctrinate.

CONCESSION

The third tactic used against Daniel—and against believers today—is to get people to concede, that is to *forfeit* something. The Jewish captives were given "a daily provision of the king's delicacies and of the wine which he drank" (Daniel 1:5). In accepting the king's food, they were asked to abandon their sacred dietary laws. The thinking was, *Why settle for kosher when you can have Chaldean?* Their goal was to make the captives' new life in Babylon so amazing they wouldn't want to go back home to Jerusalem. Nebuchadnezzar brought in the best caterers— food fit for a king!

No doubt the teenage captives in Babylon were awestruck as they saw the city surrounded by walls three hundred feet high, eighty-five feet thick, and fifty miles long.[5] Think of their amazement as they beheld in the center of the city the magnificent Hanging Gardens of Babylon, one of the Seven Wonders of the Ancient World. They could stroll through the highly adorned Ishtar Gate onto a boulevard over half a mile long. The sidewalks flanking the boulevard were made of stately red and yellow stones.[6] Paris's Champs-Élysées has nothing on the streets of Babylon.

What could have run through the minds of the young foreigners in such a situation? *Wow! This is remarkable. We're being treated like royalty here. Our God didn't protect us from these Babylonians when they conquered and burned our city. He didn't keep us from getting abducted, despite the prayers of our most pious people. Maybe He's not real; maybe everything we grew up believing isn't true.* If they embraced Babylonian food, architecture, and history, the captives would be persuaded to concede their old way of life and embrace a whole new lifestyle.

Growing up in Southern California, I watched this kind of mind-shift time and time again as people from all over the world relocated to "the land of promise." Newcomers immediately became enamored by the pull of Hollywood, the beach scene, and all the amenities and perks that come with a large coastal population. And many gladly surrendered their previously held beliefs in order to fit in and have fun.

CONFUSION

This final tactic was also the final straw intended to break the captives' will. The Babylonians took away the most personal thing anyone can possess—their names (Daniel 1:7). This change of name was intended ultimately to bring a change of identity. Daniel, which means "God is my Judge," was changed to Belteshazzar, which means "May Bel protect the king." Daniel was no longer God's namesake. His new name honored a new deity—Bel, a Babylonian god. Hananiah, whose Hebrew name means "Beloved of the Lord," was given the name Shadrach, which means "Illumined by the Sun-god, Ra." Mishael, whose name means "Who is like God?" was renamed Meshach, which means "Who is like Aku?"—referring to the Babylonian sun goddess. Azariah, "The Lord is my help," was given the name Abed-Nego, which means "Servant of the shining one." Nego, or Nebo, was another of the Babylonian gods.[7]

Imagine being swept away to a foreign land, programmed to accept new cultural standards, giving up your heritage and giving in to forbidden things. On top of it all, you were no longer the person you thought you were—you had a new name that represented a new worship system. It was brainwashing at its best. Talk about confusing! For Daniel and his friends, life had happened unexpectedly and the world demanded conformity to its status quo. How could they possibly defy their new culture's ideas and lifestyle? The downward pull of gravity was strong in Babylon.

CONQUERING INNER SPACE

Star Trek used to tell us that space was the final frontier. This iconic show promoted the idea that earthbound humans want to defy gravity by boldly going "where no man has gone before." Each episode featured the starship *Enterprise* taking a jaunt to some far-flung area of the galaxy. But defying the sort of spiritual gravity we find all around us in this fallen world requires that we "boldly go" in a different direction—conquering our inner space: our hearts and minds. Daniel made a bold choice to follow the one true God and boldly went where most other captives feared to go. He did this by taking a stand that could have cost him his life.

Scripture tells us:

> Daniel purposed in his heart that he would not defile himself with the portion of the king's delicacies, nor with the wine which he drank; therefore he requested of the chief of the eunuchs that he might not defile himself. (Daniel 1:8)

The outward pressure encountered by Daniel resulted in an inward resolve. The chief of the eunuchs was rightly afraid of the consequences for allowing Daniel to forgo the king's delicacies. This refusal might be perceived as rebellion. So Daniel reached an agreement with the man in charge of him and his friends. He took a ten-day challenge. Here's how it happened:

> Now God had brought Daniel into the favor and good-will of the chief of the eunuchs. And the chief of the eunuchs said to Daniel, "I fear my lord the king, who has appointed your food and drink. For why should he see your faces looking worse than the young men who are your age? Then you would endanger my head before the king."
> So Daniel said to the steward whom the chief of the eunuchs had set over Daniel, Hananiah, Mishael, and Azariah, "Please test your servants for ten days, and let them give us vegetables to eat and water to drink. Then

let our appearance be examined before you, and the appearance of the young men who eat the portion of the king's delicacies; and as you see fit, so deal with your servants." So he consented with them in this matter, and tested them ten days. (Daniel 1:9–14)

I'm sure you realize Daniel's decision probably didn't go over very well with the other cadets in school. They may have thought, *Great! The religious nut has taken away the king's menu and left us with vegetables and water.* But Daniel "purposed in his heart" (1:8). His resolve was deep, personal, and unwavering. He made a decision deep within himself to do what was right regardless of the consequences or what others thought. This key choice unlocked the door of effective service that would last his lifetime. Everything else in Daniel's future depended on this. Nothing else he did mattered as much as this, and had he not made this singular choice, he would not have influenced the nation as he did. Through this one decision, Daniel became the man who would soar above the status quo and impact lives for God, all because he chose to "not defile himself" (1:8).

So what does it mean to "defile yourself" today? It means to become corrupted or polluted, to be tainted by ungodly things in life. Daniel was okay with living in Babylon; he found no problem learning the language and history. Apparently he didn't care about the name change either. He knew who he really was as his identity was secure in God. Besides, history remembers him as Daniel, not Belteshazzar. He was also willing to serve the king with diligence and integrity. But he drew the line when it came to what he would eat, and here's why: Daniel was Jewish. There were certain foods prohibited by Jewish law, spelled out in the book of Leviticus. In addition, history tells us that the foods in Babylon were sacrificed to idols in the pagan temples before they reached the king's table. For Daniel, this meant that to eat this food was to partake in idolatrous worship. So he drew the line at defiling himself in this way. His choice was to love God more than food, to love God more than his new wardrobe, to love God more than his university training. In short, Daniel chose to love and obey God above anything or anyone else.

Some reading this might think, *What's the big deal? Daniel was over five hundred miles away from home. Nobody would see him.* Why not adopt the attitude, like Las Vegas, that "What happens in Babylon, *stays* in Babylon"? Or they might think, *Daniel was being too legalistic and narrow-minded.* But Daniel wasn't a legalist. He simply knew where to draw the line. Why? Because Daniel was a man of character and conviction. He cultivated those things through disciplined self-control. He wasn't looking for an excuse to sin, because he had a higher purpose to fulfill. People without purpose are always looking for an excuse to behave badly. Yet, as evangelist Billy Sunday once reportedly said, an excuse is the skin of a reason stuffed with a lie. Daniel lived with inward purpose. Living with inward purpose is always the first step in defying worldly gravity and rising above normal.

The very idea of self-control suggests a battle is taking place. Indeed, this is the case. The apostle Paul declared that our old sinful nature loves to do evil, while our new spiritual nature, which is given to us when Christ becomes our Lord, yearns for righteousness. These two forces are in conflict and the battleground is *inside of us!* Self-control is listed as the fruit (or evidence) of the Spirit in Galatians 5:22–23.

In the New Testament, self-control was used to describe athletes. Like today, successful competitors in Paul's day abstained from unhealthy diets and opted for rigorous training exercises. Holy Spirit-enabled self-control happens when you control your desires and don't allow them to control you. Why is this characteristic included as part of the fruit of the Spirit? It's simple. Self-control demonstrates that we operate by principle rather than desire. It shows that our appetites are not in the driver's seat, but God is.

But how did Daniel know where to draw the line? We can safely assume Daniel had been brought up in a godly home where the laws of the true God were honored. He had been trained to turn his heart toward God, and this is what fueled his conviction. The book of Proverbs tells us, "Keep your heart with all diligence, for out of it spring the issues of life" (Proverbs 4:23). Soaring spiritually begins with the choices you make deep in your heart, based on the Word of God.

So what defiles *you* and threatens your loyalty to God? Certain books you read? Magazines you look at? Television shows you allow in your home? Maybe it's the company you keep or relationships you toy with. You could be opening yourself to defilement by the websites you visit, the songs you download, or the episodes you watch. Have you ever decided what things you will say *no* to? When do you become deliberate about what you won't allow into your life? Where is the line you have drawn?

Why not stop for a moment and make that watershed commitment to defy the status quo and honor God in your life choices? If the lines of your life choices have become blurred, ask God to help you see clearly again. Like Daniel, purpose in your heart to avoid defilement. Live your life with the awareness that though no one else may be looking, God is always watching. Though your reputation is what you are on the outside, your character is who you are when no one is looking. You develop purpose and character—your inner space—when you resolve to honor God in your heart.

COUNT ON COMMENDATION

One of my favorite passages of Scripture says, "The eyes of the LORD run to and fro throughout the whole earth, to show Himself strong on behalf of those whose heart is loyal to Him" (2 Chronicles 16:9). God is loyal to those who are loyal to Him. In other words, God honors loyalty. His response and reward may not be immediate, but they will happen. Here's how God honored the loyalty of Daniel and his three friends:

> As for these four young men, God gave them knowledge and skill in all literature and wisdom; and Daniel had understanding in all visions and dreams.
>
> Now at the end of the days, when the king had said that they should be brought in, the chief of the eunuchs brought them in before Nebuchadnezzar. Then the king interviewed them, and among them all none was found like Daniel, Hananiah, Mishael, and Azariah; therefore they served before the king. And in all matters of wisdom and understanding about which the king examined them, he found them ten times better than the magicians and astrologers who were in all his realm. (Daniel 1:17–20)

Daniel was about twenty years old when he completed the king's college. When he and his three buddies were brought in for an interview with King Nebuchadnezzar, they stood out from the other students by exhibiting natural aptitude, intellectual acumen, and supernatural favor. They proved to be measurably superior to their contemporaries. Clear, logical thought was demanded of the new graduates, and they exhibited it in abundance! Despite their dire situation, these young Jewish men honored God, and God in turn honored them in three ways.

BENEVOLENCE

When your inner convictions result in outward obedience, God may honor you with goodwill from key people. "God had brought Daniel into the favor and goodwill of the chief of the eunuchs" (Daniel 1:9). This didn't mean life was perfect or easy for Daniel—in fact, he faced enormous opposition later on. The enemies of God would see God's favor on Daniel's life and conspire against him. But God was behind the scenes, working on Daniel's behalf. He gave Daniel favor, even in the enemy camp, calling to mind the proverb that says, "When a man's ways please the LORD, He makes even his enemies to be at peace with him" (Proverbs 16:7).

PROMINENCE

These young students graduated at the top of their class, considered by the king to be "ten times better" than their peers (Daniel 1:20). In Hebrew, the phrase is "ten hands better." The idea is that one of the four Hebrew boys was worth ten of the other guys. They were valuable in the kingdom.

INFLUENCE

We are told, "Daniel continued until the first year of King Cyrus" (Daniel 1:21). Cyrus came on the scene in 536 BC. Daniel was taken captive in 605 BC. Throughout his life—seventy years in captivity—Daniel influenced four separate kings and their court officials: Nebuchadnezzar I; Nebuchadnezzar II, also called Nabonidus; Belshazzar, the grandson of Nebuchadnezzar; and when the realm was overtaken by the Medes and Persians, Daniel influenced Cyrus the Great. Daniel impacted four world-governing rulers. That's longevity!

But Daniel didn't only influence the kings. God used him to influence others. Every Christmas we talk about the interesting characters who came from the East called Magi, who followed the star and came to Bethlehem to find the King—you know the story. History tells us the Magi were a priestly caste of Medes from Babylon. Astounding! Babylonian wise men, Medo-Persian priests, went looking for the Jewish Messiah. How on earth did they know to be on the lookout for the coming Ruler? Most scholars agree that Daniel left a legacy of his knowledge of things to come in the courts of Nebuchadnezzar, Belshazzar, and Cyrus. Daniel and these wise men still point us to the Messiah born in the manger.

COME OUT OF YOUR COMFORT ZONE

We all have a comfort zone when it comes to our place in the world. We tend to barricade ourselves behind physical and emotional comforts. But God doesn't call us to be comfortable—and let's face it, self-control isn't always comfortable. These comfort zones are a lot like blind spots; we don't even know they are there until someone points them out to us. My challenge to you is to break out of your comfort zone, to rise above the status quo by refusing to settle into a dangerous coziness.

To do so you must begin with self-control—an inward, personal resolve to honor God as a spiritual athlete. Why not even practice some self-denial? Occasionally refrain from something that is all right to do, just to remind yourself who is in charge. Remember that self-control is a way to demonstrate that you are under the direct supervision of God's will. You are showing others, as well as yourself, that God has set up camp in your heart and is calling the shots.

Lasting success can come only when you exhibit a determined and tenacious resolve that is willing to risk everything. Daniel "purposed in his heart" to defy the normal way of life. Uncomfortable? Yes! Risky? Certainly! But was it rewarding? Unquestionably! Self-control is the outgrowth of a life that is convinced of God's control. You really cannot divide your life into the sacred versus the secular. These two are interconnected. What you do in the daily mundane things of life is a window into your spiritual world. Place God in control of everything and such a commitment will show itself in self-control.

> Self-control is the outgrowth of a life that is convinced of God's control.

If you find this difficult to do on your own, get a friend to help. Daniel wasn't totally isolated, as he had his three friends to give him strength and keep him accountable. Adding a friend to the process can fortify your resolve. Ask your friend to be perfectly honest about what he or she sees as your weaknesses and strengths. Admit your weaknesses. Announce that you want to move to a deeper level spiritually and lean on your friend for encouragement and support. Accept correction. Correction will help you develop self-control by showing you what you need to avoid and where you need to improve.

You will only conquer your inner space by committing your heart, mind, and soul to God, and inviting others to help you. Then you'll find purpose and a life of influence as Daniel did. And you will be on your way to defying normal!

DARE TO DEFY N⁰RMAL: SELF-CONTROL

The Bible has a lot to say about the importance of self-control. Although the New Testament is filled with verses extolling the virtue of dedicating every part of your life to God, Solomon hit the nail on the head: "A man without self-control is like a city broken into and left without walls" (Proverbs 25:28 ESV)—unprotected and vulnerable to temptation's traps. My challenge to you is to rise up and be counted, to stand out in your self-control, and above all, to be pleasing to God.

- *Deliberate*: The battle for self-control is best fought with God as your commanding officer. Before you can conquer your inner space, you have to surrender to God's control of your entire life. Once you've done that, you can understand the real battle between your old nature and the new nature you have in Christ.

- *Defy Normal*: Read Galatians 5:16–25. Self-control is the ability to rule or regulate your personal life so that you are neither driven nor dominated by your fleshly desires. Ultimately it is a work of the Holy Spirit. Notice that the apostle Paul, in the book of Galatians, described self-control as the *fruit of the Spirit*, not the fruit of the Christian. Describe the battle every believer in Christ faces. Which aspects of your old nature present a struggle for you? Which aspects of the fruit of the Spirit have shown up in your life? How often do you pray, asking God to help you fight the old and enable the new? Plug in to His power each day—it's the only way you'll be able to defy normal and conquer your inner space.

- *Deliberate*: Most of life's greatest challenges are unexpected. However, those challenges also provide most of life's opportunities to grow. What unexpected events have you experienced?

- *Defy Normal*: Read Romans 8:28–32, Philippians 1:12, and Genesis 50:20. Take a closer look at some unexpected events from your life. First, list the facts—the what, how, where, and when of what happened. Then, look at the spiritual side—the *why* of each event. Try to understand each unexpected event in light of the following questions:

◻ How has this event challenged your relationship with God?

◻ Looking back, can you see God working behind the scenes? If so, how?

◻ Through this event, what has God shown you about Himself? About you?

◻ What might God have been doing in allowing this event to happen?

- *Deliberate*: Consider the four ways the world attempts to make you conform to the status quo: isolation, indoctrination, concession, and confusion. Sometimes it's obvious when these are happening; at other times, they are quite subtle. If you don't know your inward purpose in life, it's hard to honor God with your outward actions. Have you slipped up in your choices lately—such as what you're looking at or who you're hanging around with? Where is your line in the sand when it comes to worldly things?

- *Defy Normal*: Read Romans 12:1–3, 16–21. List the ways these verses show you how you can resist the ways of the world. A lot of it comes down to doing what is easy versus doing what is right. What would your life look like if you were willing, like Daniel, to purpose in your heart to do what is right before God, regardless of the pull of the world?

◻ Write down your commitment—your line in the sand—and post it in a place where you can see it daily: for example, your bathroom mirror, refrigerator door, or steering wheel.

- *Deliberate*: Consider the ways God honors those who honor Him: benevolence, prominence, and influence. When we commit to conquering our inner space and follow that commitment with action, God will give us opportunities to learn, grow, and serve Him in places we can't even imagine—with people we know whose attention we never thought we'd have, or with people we've never met but with whom God has arranged a divine appointment. But you'll never know what God has for you unless you break out of your comfort zone.

- *Defy Normal*: Ask a trusted friend to shoot straight with you about your strengths and weaknesses. Tell your friend you are committing to a deeper relationship with God and you want his or her support. In addition to your friend's input, ask God to show you what you need to work on, realizing that He will answer that prayer by taking you out of your comfort zone. Meet with your friend regularly to check in on your ups and downs.

CHAPTER TWO

RISK OR N⁰ REWARD

FAITH

I love the water. I overcame my fear of swimming when I first jumped off the diving board, and afterward life had no boundaries. I learned the rewards were well worth the risk. Eventually I faced the Pacific Ocean, where I took up surfing. This soon became my world. It would be the closest I'll ever get to walking on water. The buoyancy of the board and momentum of the swelling waves behind it created an exhilaration I had never known before. The water became a friendly force, one I was in sync with and one that propelled me into hours of fun. As Dana Brown put it in his documentary about surfing, I was stepping into liquid,[1] utilizing balance and gravity as a means to endless hours of delight. I learned to find my center of gravity toward the tail of the surfboard. My goal was to catch the wave just as it was breaking—when it reached maximum velocity. Then I'd feel the board carry me along the wave's momentum. Sometimes life feels that way, doesn't it? The waves of life crash against us and we need to find our center of gravity in God.

The young captive Daniel found himself in an ocean of crisis. Wave after wave seemed to crash against him: deportation, isolation, and indoctrination. He was facing a possible death sentence and he needed to make a choice. So he decided to step up and step out, finding his center of gravity in God's sovereign purpose. He put his faith on the line by trusting in the Lord at a very strategic time.

WHAT IS FAITH?

When we talk about taking a leap of faith, we're not referring to what some philosophers call a blind leap into the dark. Some people think trusting God is believing or accepting something intangible and without any substantive evidence. But trusting God is not that at all! In reality, faith is a very calculated commitment based on truths we know about God. The subjective choice to take a step of faith is based on the objective realities of God's proven character and historical track record. Like a surfer who has studied the waves and knows that standing on the board will thrust him forward because he's done it before, trusting God is a premeditated and carefully considered choice. This is the step that Daniel and his friends took—a step of real faith. Real faith is betting your life on Jesus Christ. But be assured, faith in God defies the typical path most people take.

Some people hear the word *faith* and say, "I'm not really a person of faith. I'm not into the idea there's a God up there." Yet we are quick to exercise faith in so many other areas of our lives. We place our faith in people every day. Think about it. You go to a doctor whose name you can't pronounce. He has degrees you don't verify. He gives you a prescription you can't read. You take it to a pharmacist you've never met who gives you a chemical compound you don't understand.[2] Yet, you don't hesitate for a second to swallow that pill. Spiritually, God is urging you, "Step up, step out, ride this wave of My plan for you." Unfortunately, we're so slow to trust Him. We think, *I can't trust the Lord. I might drown!*

> Real faith is betting your life on Jesus Christ.

What's wrong with us?

THE KING WHO COULDN'T SLEEP

Daniel's crisis of faith unfolded in three scenes. The first scene took place in Nebuchadnezzar's bedroom, where the king suffered from a bad case of insomnia. The story unfolds:

Now in the second year of Nebuchadnezzar's reign, Nebuchadnezzar had dreams; and his spirit was so troubled that his sleep left him. Then the king gave the command to call the magicians, the astrologers, the sorcerers, and the Chaldeans to tell the king his dreams. So they came and stood before the king. And the king said to them, "I have had a dream, and my spirit is anxious to know the dream." (Daniel 2:1–3)

Have you noticed that power has a price tag? Shakespeare wrote, "Uneasy lies the head that wears a crown."[3] Nebuchadnezzar had made it to the top, but he was in a state of high anxiety. The cares of the day became the fears of the night. You know, once you're king of the hill like Nebuchadnezzar, you start wondering how long it will be before someone tries to make a power grab, topple you off the hill, and seize your throne. Like many people, deep in the night, Nebuchadnezzar lay awake and worried.

A minister asked a boy, "Young man, do you say your prayers at night?" The boy answered, "Yes sir, I do." The minister said, "Well, do you say your prayers in the morning?" To which the boy replied, "No sir, I don't. I ain't scared during the daytime."

Have you noticed how our fears seem to loom larger in the dark of night?

Nebuchadnezzar may have worried during the day, but he was petrified at night and thus took his problems to bed. He was in that dream state where the wild things are. You know what it's like when you're trying to fall asleep and all the things you have put at bay come to haunt you. What should have been a place of rest for the king became a place of torment.

To understand Nebuchadnezzar's fears, it might help to

understand Nebuchadnezzar the man and king. Nebuchadnezzar was the oldest son of Nabopolassar, who founded the Babylonian Empire. Nabopolassar passed the empire on to his son Nebuchadnezzar, who fought many great battles, one of them being the strategic battle that brought the captives, including Daniel, to Babylon. Nebuchadnezzar was known for his cruelty. When he took King Zedekiah captive, he killed Zedekiah's sons in front of him, gouged out his eyes, and put him in chains before carrying him to Babylon (2 Kings 25:7) so that the last visual memory he had before becoming a slave was seeing his sons die.[4] This is the king who built the fiery furnace and threatened to throw people in if they didn't bow to his image (Daniel 3).

Some people hear this and say, "Wow, kings sure are temperamental." In Nebuchadnezzar's case, he was 90 percent temper and 10 percent mental. He was a reactionary, violent man. I've found that the people who harm others rightly fear that others will harm them. Fear can become a tyrant and turn those who have it into tyrannical characters. This fear is often an emotional response to uncertainty and insecurity regarding what the future may hold, and Nebuchadnezzar's world was filled with international uncertainty and political intrigue. The world empires tightened and loosened constantly. New threats were always on the transnational horizon. There was a constant ebb and flow of power. Therefore, he was a powerful yet paranoid ruler.

For two years Nebuchadnezzar and Nabopolassar served as coregents of the Babylonian Empire. But when Nabopolassar died, he left Nebuchadnezzar in charge. Nabopolassar named Nebuchadnezzar "O Nabu [Nebo], protect the son."[5] Nabu was one of the chief gods of Babylon. He was known as the god of wisdom.[6] In essence, Nabopolassar was saying, "O Nabu, god of wisdom, protect my son."

What's interesting is that Nebuchadnezzar found out that his god didn't have the wisdom to protect him or to unlock the meaning of his troubled dream. The word "troubled" used to describe Nebuchadnezzar (Daniel 2:1) means "to press" or "to beat upon." This guy was disturbed, uneasy, unsettled, and worried. And God used this to get his attention. God has ways of doing that. If He can't get our attention during the day, He might sneak in at night. Here, God spoke through a dream.

Every human being dreams. In fact the average adult dreams up to five times a night. Ninety minutes after you fall asleep, you begin your first dream, and then dreams recur about ninety minutes apart with increasing longevity.[7] Dreaming occurs when the large brain cells in the brain stem spontaneously fire, sending stimuli to the brain's cortex. Your brain tries to make sense of the stimuli by creating images (or dreams). In this case, God directed the cortical stimulation and spoke to Nebuchadnezzar through a dream.

Throughout the Bible, God used dreams to speak messages

or direct people's lives. That's not to suggest that all dreams are heavenly messages. But there *are* examples of God-directed dreams in Scripture. When Jacob ran away from home, he went to sleep on a rock at Bethel and dreamed of a ladder that reached heaven with angels of God ascending and descending on it (based on Genesis 28:12). As a young man, Joseph (one of Jacob's sons) dreamed about his future influence (Genesis 37:5–7, 9). Later, he interpreted the Pharaoh's dreams and rose to prominence in Egypt (Genesis 41:25–36). Solomon went to Gibeon and had a dream where God offered, "Ask! What shall I give you?" (1 Kings 3:5). Wouldn't that be a great dream? Of course, one of the most famous dreams was when an angel appeared to Mary's fiancé, Joseph, announcing the birth of Jesus, affirming that He would "save His people from their sins" (Matthew 1:21).

God has many ways to speak to human beings. He can break through in our dreams. He can speak through our friends' conversations, a counselor's advice, the providential alignment of our circumstances, and especially through the precepts and principles found in His written Word. To Elijah God spoke in a "still small voice" (1 Kings 19:12). To Saul of Tarsus He spoke accompanied by blinding brightness (Acts 9:3–4; Acts 22:6–8). What will it take to get through to you? God wants your attention just as He wanted Nebuchadnezzar's attention. Does He have it?

THE SEERS WHO COULDN'T SEE

No one dared defy King Nebuchadnezzar of Babylon. He was ruthless with anyone who opposed him. This king surrounded himself with people eager to please him and tell him what he wanted to hear. Though they were called his advisers and consultants, they were really sycophants.

This situation brings up an important thought: be careful who you listen to for advice. David assured us that we will be much happier ("blessed") if we don't take unwise counsel (Psalm 1:1). An old Danish proverb states, "He who builds according to every man's advice will have a crooked house."[8] Nebuchadnezzar wasn't about to let just *anyone* give him guidance. He knew that advice was like medicine. It's good to take it, but it must be the right kind—and with too much, you can overdose!

The scene shifted from the king's bedroom to the king's courtroom. After his troubled night, Nebuchadnezzar faced a testy day and called for "the magicians, the astrologers, the sorcerers, and the Chaldeans" (Daniel 2:2). In a courtly manner these advisers addressed the sleepless king:

> The Chaldeans spoke to the king in Aramaic, "O king, live forever! Tell your servants the dream, and we will give the interpretation."
>
> The king answered and said to the Chaldeans, "My decision is firm: if you do not make known the dream to

me, and its interpretation, you shall be cut in pieces, and your houses shall be made an ash heap. However, if you tell the dream and its interpretation, you shall receive from me gifts, rewards, and great honor. Therefore tell me the dream and its interpretation."

They answered again and said, "Let the king tell his servants the dream, and we will give its interpretation."

The king answered and said, "I know for certain that you would gain time, because you see that my decision is firm: if you do not make known the dream to me, there is only one decree for you! For you have agreed to speak lying and corrupt words before me till the time has changed. Therefore tell me the dream, and I shall know that you can give me its interpretation."

The Chaldeans answered the king, and said, "There is not a man on earth who can tell the king's matter; therefore no king, lord, or ruler has ever asked such things of any magician, astrologer, or Chaldean. It is a difficult thing that the king requests, and there is no other who can tell it to the king except the gods, whose dwelling is not with flesh."

For this reason the king was angry and very furious, and gave the command to destroy all the wise men of Babylon. So the decree went out, and they began killing the wise men; and they sought Daniel and his companions, to kill them. (Daniel 2:4–13)

Now that's government control! This monarch was done with formalities; he wanted results. If his clairvoyants couldn't produce, then they didn't need to be on the payroll. As shocking as this sounds, all this was actually a divine setup to move Daniel into the king's courtroom. Daniel was about to learn that God was weaving all things together.

Corrie ten Boom, who survived the atrocities of the Nazi death camps, shared this anonymous poem in her book *Tramp for the Lord:*

> My life is but a weaving,
> Between my God and me,
> I do not choose the colors
> He worketh steadily,
> Oftimes He weaveth sorrow,
> And I in foolish pride,
> Forget He sees the upper
> And I the under side.[9]

The ancient prophets were called seers, because it was believed they could see into the future. But in this case, the Chaldean seers couldn't see very well. Though "Chaldean" was an ethnic designation for people who lived in Babylon (Nebuchadnezzar was Chaldean), it was also a job description referring to the people placed in charge of the royal court. The passage also refers to magicians, who were the sacred scholars.

The astrologers were a class of priests called *magoi*, or as the New Testament calls them, the *Magi*. The sorcerers were people who used herbs, charms, and potions to foretell the future. Nebuchadnezzar called for the cream of the occult crop, but they had nothing to offer. Like a modern New Age convention, these people stood in front of the king with all the tricks of their trade, but they couldn't perceive what the king saw in his dream. They even admitted, "There is not a man on earth who can tell the king's matter" (2:10).

Years ago, before I gave my life to Christ, I dabbled in the occult. I was intrigued with astral projection and the paranormal, including autohypnosis and spirit writing. I engaged in these activities because it gave me a sense of empowerment and personal control.

A recent poll revealed that, while the majority of Americans say they believe in the basic concepts of the Bible, there is a growing interest in other spiritual practices. For example, 42 percent of those polled say they believe in ghosts, 29 percent believe in astrology, and 24 percent believe in reincarnation. In the United States 125 million people believe in astrology. Seventy percent of those read their horoscopes every single day for direction. In fact, 7 percent have said they have altered their decisions based on an astrological reading.[10] Think about that— millions of people change their decisions based upon what the stars supposedly say!

What's most alarming is growth in such beliefs among

people who claim to be Christians. According to a Pew Research Center study, 25 percent of Christians believe in astrology to some degree. Another 15 percent have consulted a psychic, 18 percent believe in ghosts, and 24 percent believe in reincarnation.[11] These statistics show that people have a true spiritual hunger. But the dream inevitably turns into a nightmare. And if you've ever changed your plans based on your horoscope or watched a psychic to gain insight into the future, I'm sure you discovered that you've been fed a bill of goods.

THE DIVINE PURPOSE OF THE CHALDEANS' FAILURE

In the court of Nebuchadnezzar these occult practices failed. But man's failure was an opportunity for God's success. Thankfully, God allowed the failure of the seers to serve some divine purposes. This failure led to three successes.

IT RATTLED THE FAITH OF THE KING

Before this divine dream encounter, the king believed in the Babylonian pantheon of deities and held to the occult worldview of the Chaldeans. He had placed his faith in the old ways of the sorcerers, magicians, and astrologers (Daniel 2:2). But when they failed to deliver, his faith in their ways was shaken. The result was that Nebuchadnezzar began thinking about the future and the future of the world after his kingdom. He didn't understand what it meant yet, but he was spiritually open. This was a good thing.

Many people don't think much about the future; they only think about the present. Most people only wonder, *What's in it for me right now?* I've heard Christians scorned as being so heavenly minded, they're no earthly good. But it's also possible to be so earthly minded that you're not much good for heavenly or earthly purposes. It's good to think about what happens after you die. You need to think about the future, because the future comes whether you like it or not.

Jesus told of a very wealthy hoarder whose future came sooner than expected. On the night he died, God said to him, "Fool! This night your soul will be required of you" (Luke 12:20). It's foolish to think only about the here and now, and not think about the future. Nebuchadnezzar was focused on the present until the Lord used a dream to rattle him and get his attention.

IT REVEALED THE FRAUD OF THE CHALDEANS

These "wise guys" couldn't produce wisdom. Dreams and omens were supposed to be their forte, but they weren't able to deliver the goods. When they said to the king, "Tell your servants the dream, and we will give the interpretation" (Daniel 2:4), what they meant was, "Tell us what the dream is and we'll make something up." But Nebuchadnezzar wanted his counselors to reveal the actual dream so he could believe the interpretation was true. He understood that if they were really in touch with the so-called gods, they could do as he asked. But the best they could come up with was something like a generic fortune cookie: "You are all-powerful. You will attain wisdom."

Back in the days when I was experimenting with occult practices, a thought occurred to me: *I'm dabbling in things I shouldn't be dealing with, but there's power here.* And then I thought, *If there's this much power on the* wrong *side, what kind of power is there on the* right *side?* I wondered what might be different if I could get in touch with real truth. One afternoon, in a San Jose apartment, I watched Billy Graham on television offer a changed life through Jesus Christ. I decided to take the faith plunge. In that instant I realized the fraudulence of my dark spiritual activities, and I stepped into the light of the knowledge of Truth (with a capital *T*).

IT RALLIED THE FERVOR OF THESE CAPTIVES

This whole situation provided the framework for Daniel and his buddies to reveal to Nebuchadnezzar that there is one true God who controls the past, present, and future. Contrary to what Nebuchadnezzar had been conditioned to believe, there was not a buffet line of many gods. There is only one God. He revealed His secrets to Daniel, and Daniel would reveal them to this king.

I think God loves to create these kinds of providential set-ups. Learn to look for them. Be open to them. Try to delight in them. That means you need to be flexible when life inconveniences you. Being taken captive was no picnic for Daniel. The years of reorientation and indoctrination were no doubt challenging to Daniel's faith. But he had the opportunity to discover why things happened as they did. All the disruptions had set the stage for Daniel's debut on the platform of God's plan for his life. This was the hour for which he was born!

THE CAPTIVES WHO COULDN'T SIT

King Nebuchadnezzar couldn't sleep well, so he woke up his wise men and made known his demands. If his staff couldn't produce the needed insight into his dream life, then he'd kill them all! Hey, you think your boss is bad? How would you like to work for a guy like that? Next time things get bothersome at your place of employment, think back to this story.

The Chaldean "seers" couldn't see—they had no idea what the king dreamed. They were as blind as bats when it came to looking into the future.

Then the scene shifted again. From the bedroom of the king and the courtroom of the kingdom, we move into the prayer room of the captives with Daniel and his buddies. These captives couldn't sit well. They were hardly passive amid the commotion. They weren't the kind of folks to just sit back and watch events happen as mere spectators. They got involved as active participants.

> The king was angry and very furious, and gave the command to destroy all the wise men of Babylon. So the decree went out, and they began killing the wise

men; and they sought Daniel and his companions, to kill them.

Then with counsel and wisdom Daniel answered Arioch, the captain of the king's guard, who had gone out to kill the wise men of Babylon; he answered and said to Arioch the king's captain, "Why is the decree from the king so urgent?" Then Arioch made the decision known to Daniel.

So Daniel went in and asked the king to give him time, that he might tell the king the interpretation. Then Daniel went to his house, and made the decision known to Hananiah, Mishael, and Azariah, his companions, that they might seek mercies from the God of heaven concerning this secret, so that Daniel and his companions might not perish with the rest of the wise men of Babylon. Then the secret was revealed to Daniel in a night vision. So Daniel blessed the God of heaven. (Daniel 2:12–19)

Notice all of the "thens" in this part of the story:
- "*Then* with counsel and wisdom Daniel answered Arioch."
- "*Then* Arioch made the decision known to Daniel."
- "*Then* Daniel went to his house, and made the decision known to Hananiah, Mishael, and Azariah."

- "*Then* the secret was revealed to Daniel in a night vision."

The phrasing suggests a pickup of step and stride. Things were happening at a breakneck pace. The angry king was going on a killing spree. Arioch, the supervisor, went to carry out the death sentence on Daniel and his friends. But what is striking is that Daniel responded rather than reacting. There was no sense of panic. An all-employee death decree had been signed and Arioch arrived with the edict, but Daniel remained cool, calm, and collected. With wisdom and poise, he basically asked, "Now, what's this all about?" Most people would try to scurry out of the palace, like the pilot who was in midflight when three of his four engines conked out. He walked out the cockpit door with a parachute on his back and said to everyone on board, "Don't worry, I'm going for help." In other words, "I'm bailing out!" But Daniel knew that when he placed his trust in God, *then* God would come through. Daniel understood that God is not the copilot; He is in total control of the flight.

What a contrast between the king and the captives. The king was sleepless, angry, and worried, while the captives were serene and calm, trusting in the Lord. I've always loved this old poem that sums up Daniel's attitude:

> Said the robin to the sparrow, "I should really
> like to know,

Why these anxious human beings rush about
   and worry so."
Said the sparrow to the robin, "Friend, I think
   that it must be,
They have no heavenly Father such as cares for
   you and me."[12]

It makes a big difference when you know the One who has
your life in His hands. You can rise above the status quo by
stepping into any situation and facing it with faith. And Daniel
stepped up in some significant ways.

DANIEL STEPPED UP BY PUTTING HIS FAITH ON THE LINE

Daniel requested a private audience in order to reveal the king's
dream and the interpretation. Nebuchadnezzar's past history
and present anxiety could have meant Daniel was about to lose
his head . . . *literally*! But that's the whole point. If Daniel did
nothing, he would die anyway. So he promised to do what no
one in the court had been able to do up to this point. Having
nothing to lose, Daniel put his faith on the line.

This reminds me of the time there was a famine in Samaria.
Four lepers were at the gate starving to death, when one of them
said, "Why are we sitting here until we die? If we say, 'We will
enter the city,' the famine is in the city, and we shall die there.
And if we sit here, we die also. Now therefore, come, let us surrender to the army of the Syrians. If they keep us alive, we shall

live; and if they kill us, we shall only die" (2 Kings 7:3–4). The lepers were spared because they took a step forward in faith.

Daniel activated his faith *in* God, because he had already abandoned his life *to* God. He knew he was safe in God's everlasting arms. Like my dad when I was standing on the diving board as a child, God was basically saying, "Step up, step out, and jump!" And Daniel said, "Done!" You see, it's one thing to say in your head, "God can do it." It's another thing to say with your actions, "God will do it—if He doesn't, I'm dead." *That's* the step of faith.

I heard about a British missionary in the 1800s named James Calvert, who boarded a ship with his family and went to the Fiji Islands, which at that time were filled with cannibals. As they came to the shore, the captain warned Calvert not to go ashore, fearing for the lives of the missionary and his family. However, exhibiting his commitment to Christ, Calvert said, "You don't understand—we died before we came. We've already surrendered our lives and deaths to our Lord." He knew he had nothing to lose and everything to gain. In a letter back to his native country of England, Calvert wrote, "I need not tell you that as heathenism gives way Christianity advances. Neither need I say that it is Christianity alone which has exposed their refuges of lies."[13]

Doesn't that sound like Daniel, who revealed the true faith found in the one true God, thus exposing the lies of the Chaldeans? It's been said that faith is putting all of your eggs in God's basket, and then counting your blessings before they hatch. That's what Daniel did. He stepped up and put his faith on the line.

How do you live out your faith? Are you willing to speak up and be unpopular and even rejected for introducing the gospel into a conversation with someone? How about when you face a financial hardship or a relational challenge? When storms come to your life, do you stay calm and unruffled? Or do you allow fear and apprehension to overpower your faith? Give these types of situations wholly over to God rather than trying to figure them out. These are times when God wants to stretch your faith. They are opportunities to become "doers of the word, and not hearers only" (James 1:22). When you step out to apply a truth or a promise from Scripture, it takes your faith to another level. Learn to put the full weight of your faith on God, knowing that He will never fail you.

> **Put the full weight of your faith on God, knowing that He will never fail you.**

DANIEL STEPPED UP BY PUTTING HIS FAITH IN THE LORD

Daniel put his faith on the line and made a commitment before man to reveal the king's dream. But he placed his faith in the Lord by calling for a prayer meeting with his friends Hananiah, Mishael, and Azariah.

I'm sure it was a lively discussion that perhaps went something like this:

Friends: "Wait, you said *what* to the king?"

Daniel: "I told him we're going to come up with the dream and the interpretation."

Friends: "You're kidding, right?"

Daniel: "Of course not! Let's pray *now!*"

This spiritual decision put their lives on the line. They had nothing to lose. So Daniel and his friends had one incredible prayer meeting. What a great picture: four young men around twenty years of age praying to the one true God in pagan, polytheistic Babylon.

THREE THINGS THAT AFFECT YOUR PRAYER LIFE

I love that prayer was these young Jews' first resort, not their last. They didn't run to the Magi to find books on dreams. They turned to prayer. Have you noticed that prayer is often our last option? We say things like, "I've tried everything else. There's nothing left to do except pray." What a sad statement! We should start with prayer. Our instinctive response to trouble should be, "Let's take this before the Lord and see what He has to say."

I've discovered that prayer life is directly proportional to three things.

YOUR PERCEPTION OF PRAYER

First, your prayer life is linked to *your perception of prayer*. A lot of people see prayer as gibberish. They think all you're doing is talking out loud or into the air, sort of like talking your confusion out loud. Or it's relegated to a feel-good ritual, like learning a catechism. To some, prayer is what you memorized as a little kid: "Now I lay me down to sleep. I pray the Lord my soul to keep." Yet the Bible asserts, "The effective, fervent prayer of a righteous man avails much" (James 5:16). "Fervent" can mean *red-hot* or something that fuels a fire. So your prayer life is directly proportional to your view of prayer. Do you see prayer as empty words, a ritualized formula, or memorized rhymes? Or do you view prayer as red-hot, passionate dialogue with your Creator? Your perception can change your reality. In other words, your uplook should change your outlook!

YOUR PERCEPTION OF GOD

Second, your prayer life is directly proportional to *your perception of God*. Many people are reticent to pray. They hesitate to pray because they wonder, *Is God in a good mood or a bad mood? Does God really even care about me?* The truth is, we approach God like we used to approach our parents, checking their mood, waiting to see if they had a good day or a bad day. A limited perception of God will alter how we approach God.

Notice that Daniel and his buddies prayed according to their knowledge of God's true character. They understood that God was in total, absolute control. They recognized that "He changes the times and the seasons; He removes kings and raises up kings" (Daniel 2:21). Daniel and his friends were "Big-Godders" rather than "Little-Godders"—that is, they knew that God was bigger than any problem they might face. And because their perception of God was so appropriately huge, they knew He could easily reveal the dream to them. He could do anything!

They also believed that God is interested in guiding people. They said, "He gives wisdom to the wise and knowledge to those who have understanding" (Daniel 2:21). Then they closed their prayer expecting an answer. In fact, they thanked Him for giving them the answer. Is that your perception of God? Your faith is only as strong as your understanding of God. I'll guarantee you that if you allow God to be to you as He is declared to be in Scripture, your faith will become indomitable. Become a Big-Godder—

> Your faith is only as strong as your understanding of God.

the type of person who lives life with faith in an unlimited, sovereign, boundless God who gladly answers prayer.

YOUR PERCEPTION OF THE PROBLEM

Third, your prayer life is directly proportional to *your perception of the problem*. Daniel and his friends understood that though they were in a dark place, God was in tune with everything going on: "He reveals deep and secret things; He knows what is in the darkness, and light dwells with Him" (Daniel 2:22). God knew what was going on and at just the right time would bring it to light.

Have you noticed that when you are hurting, you tend to pray differently? We pray more intensely when life is harder. No wonder, then, that God allows a number of heartaches and trials to come our way. He knows we need Him. Too often we don't acknowledge that need until life gets really hard. Your perception of prayer, your perception of God, and your perception of the problem will determine *what* you pray, *if* you pray, and *how often* you pray.

Daniel and his friends were in a grave situation. But they stepped up and they stepped out. They trusted God by putting their faith on the line and their trust in the Lord. And they didn't sink—they swam. In fact, they rode the wave. And God answered their prayer.

My challenge to you is to step up, step out, and see what happens. Talking to people about God, that's evangelism. Talking to God about people in prayer, that's intercession.

GET OUT OF YOUR COMFORT ZONE

I know it may make you feel awkward or vulnerable, but get out of your comfort zone. Begin by getting alone with God. Here's the secret: if you can bow before God, then you can stand before people. When you bow before God, you'll find your center of gravity. With the strength you derive from God, like Daniel and his buddies, you can step up and step out in faith anywhere in the world.

A graduating class found some resourceful ways to step out in faith. The *Chicago Tribune* reports:

It was not the words graduating senior Ryan Brown spoke at Washington Community High School commencement services on Sunday [May 21, 2001] that resonated in this small town just outside of Peoria. It was what he did before he spoke. Walking to the podium inside the gymnasium as a scheduled speaker, Brown paused, stepped to the side of the stage, folded his hands and bowed his head in a silent prayer. The gymnasium crowd of more than 1,000 students and adults erupted in cheers, with some standing to applaud while others blew air horns in celebration.

For the first time in this school's 80-year history, no prayer was heard publicly during graduation services, following a federal judge's ruling last week prohibiting it after the class valedictorian, Natasha Appenheimer, and her family obtained a temporary restraining order against the public school district.

But Brown, and other graduates who supported an invocation and benediction, did what they could to bring God into the services. Some used tape to write out messages such as "Let's Pray" and "Amen" on their caps, while others displayed crosses around their necks that were distributed by fellow students before the ceremony.

Even during his speech, Brown faked a sneeze, to which many students shouted, "God bless you."[14]

Now, that's what I call creative!

Why don't you ask God for creative ways to talk to people about God, and go often to your knees to talk to God about them? Just as Daniel did, activate your faith and step into situations believing that the Lord will use you as an agent to make your world different. The rewards will so far outweigh the risks that you'll wonder why you didn't step it up sooner.

DARE TO DEFY N⁰RMAL: FAITH

Placing your faith in God is not a blind leap but an informed choice. Daniel's story shows what real faith looks like—faith in the midst of loss and crisis and fear, faith focused on God rather than troubles. I dare you to step up to life's difficulties and use them as spiritual opportunities.

- *Deliberate*: What are some ways you exercise faith every day, generally speaking? What comes to your mind when you read the phrase *leap of faith*? Have you ever taken one? Have you ever had a chance to take a leap of faith but *not* taken it? In what ways does your view of God affect your faith?
- *Defy Normal*: List words and phrases that come to mind when you think of God. Then compare your list with the following list of God's attributes found in the Bible: eternal, merciful, good, faithful, mighty, all-powerful,

all-knowing, always present, holy, gracious, righteous, unchanging, just, loving, sovereign. What similarities and differences do you see? Are there areas where you need to align your idea of God with what the Bible says about Him? How does knowing those things about God affect your willingness to trust Him?

- *Deliberate*: The difference between passive and active faith is the difference between hearing and doing. There is no better time to put your faith into action than during a crisis.

- *Defy Normal*: Create a crisis plan for the next challenge to your faith. That challenge could be an illness, the loss of a job, or something you couldn't possibly anticipate. Your plan doesn't have to be elaborate; in fact, the simpler it is, the better. List what you know about God—His faithfulness, sovereignty, and love, for starters. Then list your part in the matter: stepping forward in faith, praying honestly and passionately to your heavenly Father, and believing that He will work in you and through you to make a difference. The next time a crisis hits, refer to your plan to remind you that God loves you and is in control.

- *Deliberate*: Real faith involves a proper perspective on God. To defy normal, you have to find your center of spiritual gravity. That happens when you step out in faith, trusting Him to be your strength and security. If you can bow before God, then you can stand before anyone. Remember, the rewards outweigh the risks.

- *Defy Normal*: Activate your faith in God and become His agent. Ask Him to use you today to have an impact on people's lives for His glory. That doesn't mean you force yourself into situations or act strangely; rather, be yourself, keep doing what you're doing with excellence and attentiveness, and trust God to set up divine appointments.

CHAPTER THREE

GO L⁰W

HUMILITY

When I travel, I usually stay at a hotel. And as most people know, hotels typically offer wake-up calls. For example, if you want to get up at four in the morning (I can't imagine why you would want to do that), you can call the lobby and they'll call your room to wake you up at four in the morning. The term *wake-up call* has become an adage in our culture, a phrase referring to a specific attention-getting event or warning sign. "It was a wake-up call," we say.

September 11, 2001, was definitely a wake-up call for our nation. It was a shocking alarm alerting us to the threat of terrorism and the need to strengthen our country's domestic security. But throughout history, there have been other "wake-up calls" as well. In 1912, when the *Titanic* took its maiden voyage through the icy waters of the North Atlantic, several surrounding ships sent messages to the ship many had dubbed "unsinkable," warning of icebergs in the water. All of those messages were wake-up calls. But you may not know that the communications officer aboard the *Titanic* wired back to one of those ships, saying, "Keep out! Shut up! You're jamming my signal."[1]

Of course, history records that the real wake-up call came at 11:40 p.m. when *Titanic* struck an iceberg and fifteen hundred lives were lost. The wake-up call went unheeded. And an opportunity was missed. The tragedy of the *Titanic* teaches us that information without appropriate action can lead to devastation.

Pride keeps people from heeding a wake-up call. Pride destroys families, ruins marriages, separates friends, and destroys churches. And pride is the one sin that will make God your instant adversary. Scripture is clear that "God resists the proud, but gives grace to the humble" (1 Peter 5:5). But just as pride is your greatest enemy, humility is your greatest friend.

A WILD PARTY

As Babylon grew in power and expanded in territory, a new king named Belshazzar found his way to the throne. He stood tall, but sadly he had forgotten what it meant to stoop, and he was about to stumble. This king possessed all the information necessary to avert a major disaster. Unfortunately, he did not listen. Like the *Titanic*'s radio operator, he was preoccupied and desperately in need of a wake-up call.

I believe God seeks to get people's attention in a number of ways—some more dramatic than others—in an attempt to avert a fatal disaster for them. Romans 13:11 exhorts, "It is high time to awake out of sleep." In Daniel 5, the alarms were definitely sounding. It was time for the king to wake up. In the middle of a lavish Babylonian cocktail party, God Himself interrupted the gathering with some divine graffiti. You may have heard the phrase *the handwriting on the wall.* Well, it comes from this story.

Here's what happened. Daniel 5:1 records: "Belshazzar the king made a great feast for a thousand

> Just as pride is your greatest enemy, humility is your greatest friend.

of his lords, and drank wine in the presence of the thousand." That was one big party. And in the middle of the festivities, a mysterious hand appeared, writing a message straight from God to Belshazzar. Interestingly, the book of Daniel was for centuries ridiculed by those in academia specifically because of this account in chapter 5. They would say, "Well, Belshazzar appears in the Bible but nowhere else in secular history. So obviously the Bible is wrong and can't be trusted." Historians claimed that Nabonidus, *not* Belshazzar, was the last king of Babylon, just prior to that kingdom falling in 539 BC. So they scoffed and laughed, saying, "Those Bible nitwits. Here's more proof you can't believe anything they say. And certainly you can't believe in a book that invents kings who never even existed!"

However, all that scoffing came to a screeching halt in 1854. During an archaeological dig in southern Iraq, a clay cylinder was discovered. Called the Nabonidus Cylinder, the cuneiform writing etched around the circumference of this object included a prayer for long life and health for King Nabonidus and his eldest son—you guessed it—*Belshazzar*. Suddenly, Belshazzar emerged out of the dirt and all the critics became strangely silent. Furthermore, in the last fifty to one hundred years archaeological discoveries have shown that not only did Belshazzar exist as the eldest son, but he was also named acting king of Babylon by his father, Nabonidus, while his father was away from the city. For fourteen of the seventeen years of his reign, Nabonidus didn't even live in Babylon. So in his place, as second-in-command, he placed Belshazzar as the king.

"Why is all that important?" you may ask. It's important because twice in Daniel 5 (vv. 7, 16) there is mention of a "third ruler" of the kingdom. "Whoever can interpret this weird thing that just happened to me," the king said, "I'll make him *third ruler* of the kingdom." But why third? Why not second? Because Belshazzar was already second in charge, and his dad was first. So whoever interpreted the handwriting on the wall earned the right to be "third." So whenever someone says, "You can't believe the Bible; it's all made up. The stories Christians claim to be history never really happened," just know they are speaking out of ignorance. In reality, the Bible has an impeccable reputation for being accurate. Every day archaeologists are digging up finds in the Middle East that validate the historical accounts found in Scripture. It has been said that archaeology is the Bible's best friend.

So back to our wild party. Daniel 5:2 says, "While he tasted the wine"—the implication here is that the king was a bit tipsy—"Belshazzar gave the command to bring the gold and silver vessels which his father Nebuchadnezzar had taken from the temple which had been in Jerusalem, that the king and his lords, his wives, and his concubines might drink from them."

"But wait," you might be saying. "I thought Nabonidus was his father." Yes, but keep in mind that the book of Daniel was written in Aramaic (including chapter 5) and in ancient Hebrew. In both of these languages, there's no word for *grandfather*. So they typically would use the word *father* to refer to an ancestor —meaning *father*, *grandfather*, and *great-grandfather*. It's the same with the word *son*. Jesus is called the "Son of David." He's not really the immediate son of David but rather a descendant of David.

So Belshazzar was partying and drinking wine with his lords, wives, and concubines, using vessels ransacked from the Jewish temple. And all the while, they were praising the "gods of gold and silver, bronze and iron, wood and stone" (Daniel 5:4). A very strange party, to say the least. But there's more. We know from history that this event took place somewhere around October 11–12, in the year 539 BC. At the same time this party was going on, Belshazzar's enemies had surrounded the walls of

Babylon. The Medes and the Persians were at the gates looking for a way to breach through the walls and overtake the city. They had already captured King Nabonidus, and now his son Belshazzar was inside, knowing he was surrounded. So what did he do? Marshal his army? Sound the alarm? No. He threw a party. A drunk-fest.

So Belshazzar the king was having fun and praising the gods of all their Babylonian belief systems. And suddenly the king had a bright idea: "Why are we drinking from these Dixie cups when we have gold and silver cups my grandfather Nebuchadnezzar stole from the Jewish temple?"

Actually it wasn't a bright idea at all, but rather a major snub in an attempt to defy the Hebrew God. And Belshazzar knew it. The practice of defying the gods of those you'd conquered was quite common in his day. Showing the superiority of the Babylonian gods was especially important in light of the fact that another nation was about to overtake them at any moment. So it was a calculated insult to the Jewish God. But it didn't hide the fact that Belshazzar the king was asleep at the wheel during the moment his entire kingdom was on the verge of being invaded and collapsing. He was trying to get all of his leaders into a drunken stupor from which they would likely never wake up.

Belshazzar could have profited from Solomon's wisdom: "It is not for kings to drink wine, nor for princes intoxicating drink" (Proverbs 31:4).

Leaders must think clearly when making decisions that affect a nation. Solomon also penned, "Wine produces mockers; alcohol leads to brawls. Those led astray by drink cannot be wise" (Proverbs 20:1 NLT). And there was a whole room full of mockers in Daniel 5.

It was a wild night in Babylon.

A WEIRD PICTURE

The book of Daniel continues the story. "In the same hour the fingers of a man's hand appeared and wrote opposite the lampstand on the plaster of the wall of the king's palace; and the king saw the part of the hand that wrote. Then the king's countenance changed, and his thoughts troubled him" (Daniel 5:5–6).

That would be an understatement. Can you imagine? But Daniel got even more specific. The appearance of the hand so disturbed Belshazzar that

> the joints of his hips were loosened and his knees knocked against each other. The king cried aloud to bring in the astrologers, the Chaldeans, and the soothsayers. The king spoke, saying to the wise men of Babylon, "Whoever reads this writing, and tells me its interpretation, shall be clothed with purple and have a chain of gold around his neck; and he shall be the third ruler in the kingdom." Now all the king's wise men came, but they could not read the writing, or make known to

the king its interpretation. Then King Belshazzar was greatly troubled, his countenance was changed, and his lords were astonished. (Daniel 5:6–9)

Several years ago I had the privilege of visiting Babylon, and we were taken into this room that was 56 feet wide by 173 feet long. That's a big room. Our archaeological guide then announced, "Gentlemen, you are standing in the very room where the handwriting on the wall appeared at Belshazzar's feast the night Babylon fell in 539 BC." And what was interesting to me was that we could see toward the bottom of the wall that was previously covered by dirt. There, we saw the plaster still on the walls, *exactly* as the Bible describes it. It was astounding.

I don't know if anyone has documented the world record for the shortest time it takes to sober up, but I would say Daniel 5 just might describe it. A hand appeared—not attached to a body or an arm—just a hand, floating in midair, writing something on the wall. The Bible vividly describes what we now know physically happened to Belshazzar in a situation like this. Upon seeing this mysterious hand, adrenaline surged into the king's body, priming the fight-or-flight reflex that often makes a person sick to his stomach, sending his heart rate into overdrive. Belshazzar was scared out of his mind! Daniel said, "The king's countenance changed . . . so that the joints of his hips were loosened and his knees knocked against each other" (Daniel 5:6). The idea is, Belshazzar couldn't even stand up—fear had drained his strength. But in this particular case, the king's fear stemmed from guilt. Sure, he knew what was happening outside the city walls. But he also knew something about his grandpa Nebuchadnezzar and how God had humbled him (Daniel 4:28–37). He was well aware of God's reputation in the kingdom of Babylon. It was well attested to in Babylonian history.

You see, when a person is guilty, he sees all of life through that lens. A guilty conscience makes cowards of us all when we're not walking right with the Lord. Remember Adam and Eve? God came to them in the cool of the day after they sinned and called for them. And when God called for them, what did they do? They ran and hid. They had never done that before. Previously, they had walked with God out in the open. But after sinning, they felt major guilt and interpreted all of life's events through that lens and perspective.

> A guilty conscience makes cowards of us all when we're not walking right with the Lord.

It was the same here with Belshazzar. He knew God was real and that he was in trouble. So he brought in all of these lame Babylonian soothsayers, and not one of them could read the inscription. And why not? Couldn't they at least read what it said? Apparently not. Some have suggested the writing was some sort of ideogram, pictogram, or cuneiform-looking figure that they were unfamiliar with. Or it could have been that God simply confused the king's wise men, hiding the meaning from them. Either way, this gives us an incredible picture of what the Bible calls the "natural man." A natural man isn't a guy who goes without deodorant or who eats granola. Rather, a natural man is who we are by nature as fallen human beings, our natural sinful state apart from Jesus Christ. And 1 Corinthians 2:14 states, "The natural man does not receive the things of the Spirit of God, for they are foolishness to him; nor can he know them, because they are spiritually discerned."

That's why unbelievers can hear a sermon, or read Scripture, and not "get it." They can't figure it out. It doesn't make sense to them. And here in Daniel 5, this handwriting contained spiritual truth, a revelation from God. But this isn't the only instance in the Bible when God wrote something.

In John 8, the Pharisees brought to Jesus a woman caught in adultery and said, "Moses, in the law, commanded us that such should be stoned. But what do You say?" (v. 5). You know what Jesus said? Nothing. Instead, He bent down and started writing on the ground with His finger. When they saw what He was writing, they all walked away. The question has always been: "What did Jesus write?" And the answer is that we don't know. Scripture doesn't say. Perhaps Jesus wrote their names and secret sins or other commandments they themselves had broken. Maybe, and it's just a thought, He wrote the same words God had previously written on Belshazzar's wall centuries earlier:

MENE, MENE, TEKEL, UPHARSIN

Translation: "MENE: God has numbered your kingdom, and finished it; TEKEL: You have been weighed in the balances, and found wanting; PERES: Your kingdom has been divided, and given to the Medes and Persians" (Daniel 5:26–28). Had Jesus written these words, it would have been a story those Jewish leaders were familiar with; they would have immediately gotten the point. But either way, the king's wise men could not decipher the handwriting, so they were petrified with fear, and for good reason.

Could there be "handwriting on the wall" in your life? Has God been trying to get your attention for a while? Maybe it's a crisis or a close call. An accident or a health scare, but you're still here. Maybe it's a family-related problem or work situation. God knows that some people only need a gentle tap on the shoulder while others require a jolt or a kick in the pants. Either way, He knows what it takes to get a person's attention. In a crisis the first question we ask is: "How can I get out of this?" But here are some better questions we should ask ourselves: "What can I get out of this?" "Is God trying to say anything to me, and if so, what?" I understand it's a paradigm shift to think this way, but doing so leads us toward maturity and Christlikeness.

A WISE PROPHET

Act 3 of this developing drama sees the queen making an appearance. But who was this queen? She couldn't have been Belshazzar's wife, because verse 2 says that all his wives were at the party drinking it up with him. More about that in a few minutes. Here's how the Bible breaks it down:

> The queen, because of the words of the king and his lords, came to the banquet hall. The queen spoke, saying, "O king, live forever! Do not let your thoughts trouble you, nor let your countenance change. There is a man in your kingdom in whom is the Spirit of the Holy God. And in the days of your father, light and understanding and wisdom, like the wisdom of the gods, were found in him; and King Nebuchadnezzar your father—your father the king—made him chief of the magicians, astrologers, Chaldeans, and soothsayers. Inasmuch as an excellent spirit, knowledge, understanding, interpreting dreams, solving riddles, and explaining enigmas were found in this Daniel, whom the king named Belteshazzar, now let Daniel be called, and he will give the interpretation."
>
> Then Daniel was brought in before the king. The king spoke, and said to Daniel, "Are you that Daniel who is one of the captives from Judah, whom my father the king brought from Judah? I have heard of you, that the Spirit of God is in you, and that light and understanding and excellent wisdom are found in you. Now the wise men, the astrologers, have been brought in

before me, that they should read this writing and make known to me its interpretation, but they could not give the interpretation of the thing. And I have heard of you, that you can give interpretations and explain enigmas. Now if you can read the writing and make known to me its interpretation, you shall be clothed with purple and have a chain of gold around your neck, and shall be the third ruler in the kingdom." (Daniel 5:10–16)

What's amazing to me is that Belshazzar, king of Babylon, either didn't know who Daniel was, or he knew who Daniel was and had completely ignored him. He certainly would have known about when his grandfather lost his mind and Daniel's strong connection to that incident. Whatever the case, Daniel was noticeably absent from this gathering, apparently not a member of the "Drunk Leaders Club." But now he was summoned into the king's presence.

Joseph Parker writes, "Preachers of the Word, you will be wanted some day by Belshazzar; you were not at the beginning of the feast, but you will be there before the banqueting hall is closed. The king will not ask you to drink wine, but he will ask you to tell him the secret of his pain and to heal the malady of his heart. Abide your time. You're a nobody now. But the preacher will have his opportunity. They will send for him when all other friends have failed."[2]

What is true of preachers is also true of every Christian. When your unbelieving friends hit a wall in life—a personal, marital, or family crisis—and they don't know where to turn, they may very likely reach out to the only Christian they know for help, advice, or even prayer. So be there for your lost friends and be ready!

Clearly, all of Belshazzar's other friends had failed him, so Daniel was brought in on the queen's recommendation. I mentioned earlier that this couldn't have been his wife, and here's why: She was most assuredly the queen mother—Belshazzar's mother, wife of Nabonidus and daughter of Nebuchadnezzar. According to history, Nabonidus married this woman, whose name was Nitocris. This marriage was what gave Nabonidus the right to rule, as he wasn't from the direct lineage of Nebuchadnezzar.

King Belshazzar made Daniel an offer of fine clothing, gold chains, and a position of great authority in the kingdom. And Daniel's response? "Let your gifts be for yourself, and give your rewards to another; yet I will read the writing to the king, and make known to him the interpretation" (Daniel 5:17).

At this point, Daniel was in his seventies or eighties. It had been a long time since he was taken captive as a teenager. He had experienced the good, bad, and ugly of life in the Babylonian empire. He'd "been there, done that." He didn't want the gold, the fame, or the position. He wasn't even tempted by it. So he replied,

O king, the Most High God gave Nebuchadnezzar your father a kingdom and majesty, glory and honor. And because of the majesty that He gave him, all peoples, nations, and languages trembled and feared before him. Whomever he wished, he executed; whomever he wished, he kept alive; whomever he wished, he set up; and whomever he wished, he put down. But when his heart was lifted up, and his spirit was hardened in pride, he was deposed from his kingly throne, and they took his glory from him. Then he was driven from the sons of men, his heart was made like the beasts, and his dwelling was with the wild donkeys. They fed him with grass like oxen, and his body was wet with the dew of heaven, till he knew that the Most High God rules in the kingdom of men, and appoints over it whomever He chooses.

But you his son, Belshazzar, have not humbled your heart, although you knew all this. (Daniel 5:18–22)

Wow. If you're a pagan king and you call for a true man of God, you should expect a sermon, not a pat on the back. Notice Daniel didn't say, "O king, live forever! Long live the king!" because he realized the king was going to die in a few hours. Daniel predicted the fall of this kingdom, so he got right to it, leveling three hefty charges against this king.

CHARGE #1: "YOU HAVE DISREGARDED KNOWLEDGE"

Daniel was saying in essence, "There are certain things you knew, and you have pushed them aside. You knew about Nebuchadnezzar your grandfather. You knew what God did to him, and how God humbled him so he would come to his senses and glorify God at the end of that. You've known *all* this, but you still blew it off. You didn't heed the wake-up call."

I believe God judges individuals and nations based on the amount of knowledge they have. You can stop worrying about the jungle natives who have never heard the gospel. I hear that all the time: "What about the people who have never heard?" But you *have* heard! I live with a different amount of light than they do. God made them, so I'll let Him worry about them. I still want to get the gospel to them, but I'm not worried. Someone says, "Well, what about the people who have never had a Bible?" I say, "But *you* have one!"

Questions like these are a way of diverting away from a person's own responsibility before God. When someone stands before God at death, the issue He will deal with will be *that person's* response to the gospel, not the response of some native living in the jungle.

What about you? How many sermons have you heard in your life? How many books like this have you read? And what about America? Will our nation be judged for the light it has? Think of the hundreds of thousands of churches, millions of

Christians, thousands of Christian radio stations, and a hundred Christian television stations, not to mention podcasts and Internet videos. Virtually all Christian truth is easily accessible today. This nation has more light than any other on the planet, and America will be judged accordingly.

Jesus lived in Galilee, but He chose Capernaum as His headquarters. There were three little villages next to each other: Capernaum, Bethsaida, and Chorazin. They each heard what Jesus said. They all saw what Jesus did. And yet they were all indifferent to it. So one day Jesus said to them,

> Woe to you, Chorazin! Woe to you, Bethsaida! For if the mighty works which were done in you had been done in Tyre and Sidon, they would have repented long ago, sitting in sackcloth and ashes. But it will be more tolerable for Tyre and Sidon at the judgment than for you. And you, Capernaum, who are exalted to heaven, will be brought down to Hades. He who hears you hears Me, he who rejects you rejects Me, and he who rejects Me rejects Him who sent Me. (Luke 10:13–16)

The Son of God was living in their town, and they totally blew Him off. And the people of those cities were judged according to the light that they sinned against. So charge number one against Belshazzar: "You've disregarded knowledge."

CHARGE #2: "YOU HAVE DEFIED THE TRUE GOD"

Daniel 5:23 says, "You have lifted yourself up against the Lord of heaven. They have brought the vessels of His house before you, and you and your lords, your wives and your concubines, have drunk wine from them." In other words, "You didn't do this in ignorance, Belshazzar. You did it in full-on defiance. You shook a scoffing fist at the same God you knew greatly humbled your grandpa."

This was some sermon Daniel delivered. Again, he was in his seventies or eighties, and he simply didn't care what people thought about him or what they might do to him. But more importantly, he had also developed a rock-solid faith in a God who would deliver His children out of lions' dens and fiery furnaces.

CHARGE #3: "YOU HAVE DEIFIED FALSE GODS"

The end of Daniel 5:23 notes, "And you have praised the gods of silver and gold, bronze and iron, wood and stone"—all the statues around Babylon—"which do not see or hear or know; and the God who holds your breath in His hand and owns all your ways, you have not glorified."

Daniel was saying, "King Belshazzar, you pray and sing to a bunch of statues that can't answer back or hear a word you're saying. That's really dumb!"

What a contrast here between the Babylonians' inanimate

statues and images and the living God who can write on a wall! I love Daniel's words: "The God who holds your breath in His hand and owns all your ways." That's quite a God! In the 1800s a man by the name of William Ernest Henley, a British humanist, secularist, and poet, penned a famous poem called "Invictus." In it, Henley writes, "I am the master of my fate: I am the captain of my soul."[3]

Daniel would disagree.

You see, at the end of the line for Henley, Belshazzar, and every person who has ever lived on earth is the God who "holds your breath in His hand and owns all your ways." What a moment this must have been!

A WEIGHTY ANNOUNCEMENT

Following his fiery message of rebuke, Daniel then proceeded to translate for the king: "And this is the inscription that was written: MENE, MENE, TEKEL, UPHARSIN" (Daniel 5:25).

No wonder the Chaldean seers couldn't interpret the message! In fact, nobody could. Nobody except wise old Daniel. And here is his interpretation: "MENE: God has numbered your kingdom, and finished it" (v. 26). Here is *my* translation: "Belshazzar, your number is up. Your days are numbered. You're done, bud. Finished."

Ironically, in just a few hours King Belshazzar would be dead. His days—make that his *hours*—were indeed numbered.

As Psalm 90:12 reminds us, "Teach us to number our days, that we may gain a heart of wisdom." James put it this way: "For what is your life? It is even a vapor that appears for a little time and then vanishes away" (4:14). Hebrews 9:27 states, "It is appointed for men to die once, but after this the judgment." The truth is that, for all of us, our days are limited and tomorrow is not promised.

The second word was "TEKEL," which means "weighed." "You have been weighed in the balances, and found wanting" (Daniel 5:27). This implies weighing something on the scale and finding it to be light. Interpreted for the king: "Belshazzar, you're a lightweight. You are all fluff and no substance."

The final word, PERES, means "divided." ("UPHARSIN" is used in Daniel 5:25. "U" is the word for "and." PHARSIN is the plural of PERES.) Thus, "Numbered, numbered, weighed, and divided." As Daniel explained in verse 28, "Your kingdom has been divided, and given to the Medes and Persians."

Meanwhile, during Daniel's sermon, outside Babylon's walls were the Medes and the Persians. They had surrounded the city, and a general named Cyrus, who worked for King Darius the Mede, came up with an ingenious idea. He knew that although Babylon was considered impregnable, the Euphrates River ran through the city. So he devised a plan to dam the river upstream, diverting it into a swamp. This would cause the city's water level to drop dramatically to about knee height, enabling the Medes and Persians to walk underneath the wall of the city and kill the guards.[4] By the time Belshazzar's party was over, the entire Persian army was inside Babylon, fulfilling Daniel's prophetic words: "Your kingdom has been divided, and given to the Medes and Persians." Scripture further records, "That very night Belshazzar, king of the Chaldeans, was slain. And Darius the Mede received the kingdom, being about sixty-two years old" (Daniel 5:30–31).

WHAT WILL YOU DO?

As there was for Belshazzar, there will be a last night and a last meal for each one of us. There is a final statement that will come from our mouth. There will be a last breath—and then eternity. In the meantime your life is being weighed in God's balances. So is it all fluff, or is it substantive? Is there integrity? Is there depth? One day you will stand, not in a party room or in a royal hall with handwriting on a wall, but rather before a divine judgment seat with handwriting in the Book of Life. Revelation 20 declares, "I saw the dead, small and great, standing before God, and books were opened. And another book was opened, which is the Book of Life. . . . And anyone not found written in the Book of Life was cast into the lake of fire" (vv. 12, 15).

Granted, this is not a pleasant thought. But here's the good news. Colossians 2:14 says that Jesus Christ has "wiped out the handwriting of requirements that was against us, which was contrary to us. And He has taken it out of the way, having nailed it to the cross." In other words, Jesus took the handwriting on the wall that said, "You're guilty. You're guilty. You're guilty!" and He nailed it to the cross. For a lot of people, on that final judgment day, the party is over. But for others, the party has just begun! For those who have humbled themselves before God, eternity will hold the biggest, coolest party ever!

What about you? Has God been trying to get your attention lately? Perhaps even through this book. Maybe you've sensed Him saying, "I love you so much. I want to invade your life and show you what I have for you." I wonder what you'll say to Him. Will you say, "Keep out! Shut up! You're jamming my signal," like the communications officer did on the *Titanic*? Will you disregard the knowledge of God that you now have, remain in your pride, and defy God to His face?

Or instead will you say, "Yes, Lord! Please take over my life right now"?

The Most High God, as Daniel accurately proclaimed, holds your breath in His hand. He owns your ways. Each breath you are taking at this very moment is one of His many gifts to you. Every heartbeat. Every sunrise. All these are gifts from a gracious God who loves you more than you can possibly imagine. My advice is to go low. Humble yourself before God.

CULTIVATE HUMILITY

Pride is the oldest sin in the universe, and it shows no signs of growing weaker with age. Pride put Lucifer out of heaven (Isaiah 14:12–15), our first parents out of the Garden of Eden

(Genesis 3:22–24), and Belshazzar out of his regency. If you're going to live above the status quo, if you're going to defy the normal flow of your culture, then go low. That's what humility means. Humility doesn't mean thinking badly of yourself or thinking unfavorably of yourself; it simply means *not* thinking of yourself at all! Just as pride is a barrier to the storehouse of God's blessing, humility unlocks that door.

Here are a few things to help you cultivate humility and produce a go-low attitude.

PRAYER

When you pray, you are demonstrating dependence. You are saying to God, "I need You. I can't and won't go it alone." Starting your mornings this way helps set the tone of reliance and helps you lean in the right direction (toward God). Prideful people don't pray. Like Belshazzar, they don't think they need God—and it shows.

GENUINE WORSHIP

Worship is all about shifting your focus. In worship we move the spotlight away from ourselves and our preoccupations and onto God. It's giving Him all the credit. In worship we recall to mind God's personality, God's provision, and God's promises.

Contrast that with the attitude of our culture—*it's all about me!* This attitude is reflected in some hard numbers. One pair of psychologists recently did the research and found a "fivefold increase in plastic surgery and cosmetic procedures in just ten years, the growth of celebrity gossip magazines, Americans spending more than they earn and racking up huge amounts of debt, the growing size of houses, the increasing popularity of giving children unique names, polling data on the importance of being rich and famous, and the growing number of people who cheat."[5] You don't need to go to any of the social media forums to discover the problem: we've replaced worshipping God with worshipping ourselves.

Narcissus was a fellow in Greek mythology who fell in love with his own reflection. He got stuck on himself while looking at his reflection in a pool of water—the first selfie?—and just stuck around, wasting away while pining over himself. Even though it's purely a story, it seems that Narcissus has produced many offspring today. One broadly applied psychological test classified 30 percent of young people as narcissistic—and noted that the number has doubled in last thirty years![6] It seems that what started as a push for self-esteem has become a flood of self-adoration. Genuine worship will cure those ills.

VOLUNTEER FOR UNDESIRABLE TASKS

When you willingly take on an activity not assigned to you or expected of you, you cultivate humility. A willingness to serve others, to bow lower than your pay grade, will remind you of your calling as a follower of Jesus Christ, and it will also inspire others to do the same.

ENCOURAGE OTHERS

You are where you are today because of someone else, and you can pass it forward to someone else. A pat on the back is only a few inches away from a kick in the pants, but it is miles ahead in results! Pouring water on someone's enthusiasm is easy and far too prevalent. The world is full of discouragers. Encouragement will keep many a man or woman on their feet, and it will keep you on your knees.

These simple practices will serve you well. They will keep you from the kind of tragedy that happened to this arrogant King Belshazzar. Our time is coming. I pray the knowledge of God that you now have won't be wasted information leading to disaster, but information that leads to *action*, which brings celebration!

If you feel empty and lonely deep within, if you just don't get it or understand all Christian truth, that's okay. But if, at the same time, there is also a craving deep inside your heart to know truth, to be satisfied, to have purpose, to be settled and not wander, then consider this very moment—right now—as your personal wake-up call from God.

DARE TO DEFY NORMAL: HUMILITY

Everyone needs a wake-up call at some point. The bigger question is, will we recognize our wake-up call when it comes? Nebuchadnezzar's dream prompted him to seek counsel, and

God used Daniel to interpret the king's dream and give him a heads-up on the future. Belshazzar, on the other hand, failed to learn from his predecessor's humbling exile to the pasture, and by the time his wake-up call came, it was too late for him—the writing was already on the wall. I dare you to humble yourself, before God does. When you do, He will lift you up and use you for His glory.

- *Deliberate*: How do you respond in a crisis? It's typical and totally natural to ask God to get you out of it. After all, who has time for trials and troubles? A humble attitude, however, recognizes that God allows such hardships, and though you might never know why, you can always trust that God can bring something good out of even the worst situation. What did Jesus do to deserve the cross? Nothing. And if He suffered, you won't be exempt. Suffering offers you a chance to be like Him, to focus on God and trust His purposes and plans.

- *Defy Normal*: What if the next time trouble rears its head, you ask yourself, "What can I get out of this? Is God trying to tell me something?" It's not a natural way to look at hardship, but it is a mark of spiritual maturity.

- *Deliberate*: God's light attracts those caught in darkness. The kings Daniel served were drawn to his faith, integrity, and godliness—even if they didn't know it was those qualities that attracted them. Everything you do to draw close to God invites attention—sometimes persecution, but also opportunity. You may be the only Christian others encounter, so be ready!

- *Defy Normal*: Make a list of unbelievers you know. Ask God to give you an opportunity to bless them—to help them in a time of need or to listen to a hard question about God. Stay close to God in prayer and in His Word, preparing yourself for the opportunities.

- *Deliberate*: Consider the three charges Daniel leveled against Belshazzar: he disregarded what he knew about Nebuchadnezzar's fall and restoration, he defied the one true God, and he deified false gods. In other words, Belshazzar thought he was the boss. With one swift move, God corrected his mistaken thinking, and the king's pride led to his fall.

- *Defy Normal*: Take some time to recount how you have changed since you became a Christian. What has God done in your life to give you peace and purpose? What old ways of thinking and behaving have you left behind? What new attitudes and actions have replaced them? When you're done, thank God for His faithful work in you. Then pray that He will give you a chance to bless someone with your story.

- *Deliberate*: Few things defy normal like going low. Pride is the default setting of the highest created beings, whether angels or people. Don't settle for selfishness; turn the focus from yourself toward God and others.

- *Defy Normal*: Cultivate humility through prayer, worship, volunteering for undesirable tasks, and encouraging others. Start with prayer and focus on God. Then list practical ways you can cultivate humility and ask God to give you opportunities to do more.

CHAPTER FOUR

FIND A HILL WORTH DYING ON

INTEGRITY

The famous lyricist Oscar Hammerstein once wrote about a photo he saw of the Statue of Liberty. A helicopter had flown over the statue and the photo was snapped from above. Hammerstein commented that he was amazed at the detail on top of the statue. "The sculptor had done a painstaking job with the lady's coiffure, and yet he must have been pretty sure that the only eyes that would ever see this detail would be the uncritical eyes of sea gulls. He could not have dreamt that any man would ever fly over this head and take a picture of it. He was artist enough, however, to finish off this part of the statue with as much care as he had devoted to her face and her arms and the torch and everything that people can see as they sail up the bay.

. . . When you are creating a work of art, or any other kind of work, finish the job off perfectly."[1]

Of all of the attributes people may possess—whether genius, brilliance, or competence—integrity tends to top the list. It's the mark of someone who undertakes a venture in the right way, with no agenda other than giving all to honor and serve God. Daniel did just that in Babylon. He was a faithful, dependable man. In fact, his faithfulness summed up his life—it was both the defining result and the source of his integrity. His life was like an ancient city with four defining walls—four "walls of integrity." Daniel practiced integrity personally, professionally, critically, and spiritually. He demonstrated unusual dependability toward his boss, his country, and his God.

THE WALL OF PERSONAL INTEGRITY

What *one* characteristic defines you? If you had to pick a single word that sums up your character, what would that word be? For some it would be *energetic*; for others *courageous* sums them up best; for others it might be *hesitant* or *pessimistic* or even *cynical*. But let me suggest that *integrity* will set you apart from the crowd faster than anything else. Integrity is doing the right thing when no one is looking but God—or, as Oswald Chambers noted, "My worth to God in public is what I am in private."[2] Daniel's integrity manifested itself in his faithfulness. Whether he was in Jerusalem or Babylon, by himself or before the king, he stayed true to what he knew was right. In fact, it's the *context* of Daniel's faithfulness that makes it so significant and worthy of imitation.

A new king and administration was now in Babylon. Nebuchadnezzar and Belshazzar were gone, their kingdom having fallen to the Medes and the Persians. The end of Daniel 5 introduces us to a new ruler named Darius the Mede. We know historically the real king was Cyrus the Persian, but it's generally thought that he used Darius as his viceroy and thus the de facto king to rule over the vast region of Babylon.[3]

> Integrity is doing the right thing when no one is looking but God.

What Nebuchadnezzar had thought impossible had finally happened: Babylon had fallen and a new kingdom had arisen—as Daniel had predicted in chapter 2.

In Daniel 6 we read,

It pleased Darius to set over the kingdom one hundred and twenty satraps [territorial leaders], to be over the whole kingdom; and over these, three governors, of whom Daniel was one, that the satraps might give account to them, so that the king would suffer no loss. (vv. 1–2)

Daniel became one of three chiefs of staff, or administrative governors, over one hundred and twenty princes or territorial rulers (satraps). The regional rulers all gave an account to three guys in charge, Daniel being one of them. By now, Daniel was about eighty-five years old. He had been in Babylon close to seventy years. The Jewish captivity was almost over. Since chapter 1, when he was a teenager, Daniel had purposed in his heart to faithfully follow God. Six kings had come and gone, and another kingdom had arisen. Yet Daniel was still there. Consistent. Still on the job, faithful, serving the Lord through all of these kings. Integrity isn't just doing the right thing once, but rather doing the right thing over and over and over and over. Daniel displayed that kind of persistent dependability and uprightness over time. You might say integrity was the soundtrack to Daniel's life.

When William Carey, the great missionary to India, announced that he wanted to go overseas and serve the Lord on the mission field, his dad wasn't excited. Carey had young children and a wife, who at that point refused to join him. When his father called him and tried to dissuade him from going, Carey replied, "I have many sacrifices to make. . . . But I have set my hand to the plough."[4]

Oh, the wonderful things God has done through faithful men and women who simply put their hands to the plow, who put one foot in front of the other and plod along faithfully and consistently over time. And here's one of the things I love about Daniel: he was eighty-five and still not retired! I'm not saying it's bad to retire, but in our culture we'd want to put Daniel in a retirement home. Our culture reveres the young and ignores the aged, when unfortunately, that's where all the wisdom lies. Daniel was still very much at work in this kingdom and for his God.

Did you know that Thomas Edison was still applying for patents into his eighties?[5] Frank Lloyd Wright drafted about one-third of his entire life's designs during the last decade of his life.[6] John Wesley at eighty-eight could still preach forcefully and articulately after having traveled thousands of miles by horseback, preaching four thousand sermons, and writing voluminously.[7] As of this writing, Billy Graham is ninety-six and continues to influence others for the kingdom. I once visited Graham's longtime song leader George Beverly Shea in his home. He was 102 at the time and could still sing better than most.

THE WALL OF PROFESSIONAL INTEGRITY

Eugene Peterson described integrity with the title of his popular book *A Long Obedience in the Same Direction*.[8] Faithful, consistent, long obedience in the same direction—that was Daniel. But he also "distinguished himself above the governors and satraps, because an excellent spirit was in him; and the king gave thought to setting him over the whole realm" (Daniel 6:3). Once again Daniel rose to a high-ranking government position, spreading a wholesome influence wherever he went, generation after generation. It's interesting that virtually every one of Daniel's bosses viewed him as somebody who was a cut above the rest, leading to promotion. God brought the teenage Daniel into the favor and goodwill of the chief of the eunuchs. Then King Nebuchadnezzar promoted him, appointing him ruler over the whole province of Babylon and the chief administrator over all the wise men. Belshazzar promoted him to become the third ruler of the kingdom. On a professional level, every boss saw his dependability and competence. His integrity made him stand out. That's something every believer should strive for.

Jesus said, "You are the light of the world. . . . Let your light so shine before men, that they may see your good works and glorify your Father in heaven" (Matthew 5:14, 16). Next to home and school, work is where you spend most of your time. You will spend half of your waking life working. Think about that. If you live to be seventy years of age, you will have worked a total of twenty solid years. That's twenty years for people to observe how you work, your ethics, and what your character is like. Daniel was in a secular job, yet he was serving the Lord—not through preaching but through performing his job well. The phrase "distinguished himself above the governors and satraps" (6:3) is rendered in the New American Standard Bible as "Daniel began distinguishing himself," indicating Daniel's behavior as something he did *regularly*. In other words, this was his work ethic. He was a hard worker, a diligent employee, a reliable representative. Whatever he did, he did well, and that consistent excellence caused him to stand out.

Do you want to be the best witness for Christ at your job? Then be the best worker. Start seeing your workplace as a place that deserves the best of who you are. And when you develop the reputation of being a hard worker, you are paving the way for open opportunities to share your faith. When you are a faithful, hardworking employee, people can rely on you. And that's both a rare and attractive quality. Daniel was that man. He distinguished himself. Daniel wasn't a griper or complainer. He didn't mope around with his head down. Even during the worst trial of his life, he still thanked God. That's an "excellent spirit" (v. 3). And this excellent spirit began with a grateful attitude.

When was the last time you thanked your boss? You may wonder, *Why should I thank my boss? I'm not getting paid enough.* Thank him or her that you have a job. And if you really don't like your job, then keep working where you are but take steps to transition elsewhere. Until then, remember this: gratitude is the attitude that sets the altitude for the Christian life. Resolve to be all in when it comes to your employment. Give it your very best. Display a thankful attitude. That's part of having an excellent spirit. Daniel possessed a fierce work ethic and an excellent spirit, no matter what job was assigned to him.

> Gratitude is the attitude that sets the altitude for the Christian life.

We see the same principle in the New Testament. In the first century, many employees were actually slaves. So with that in mind, look at Paul's counsel in Ephesians 6:

Bondservants [also translated "slaves"], be obedient to those who are your masters according to the flesh, with fear and trembling, in sincerity of heart, as to Christ; not with eyeservice, as men-pleasers, but as bondservants of Christ, doing the will of God from the heart, with goodwill doing service, as to the Lord, and not to men, knowing that whatever good anyone does, he will receive the same from the Lord, whether he is a slave or free. (vv. 5–8)

Paul encouraged slaves who had become Christians to show themselves to be humble, hardworking, and subservient to their slave owners so that they could promote Christ's message. That's the same message Daniel exemplified. Work hard and have a great attitude. Integrity means wholeness in all you do—you are the same on Friday night as you are Sunday morning. If every Christian took that attitude to work on Monday morning, it would transform businesses all across the country, turning a job of drudgery into meaningful ministry. If Jesus is your greatest joy, then it will spill over into your work. Your work will then open the door for your words to have the greatest impact.

THE WALL OF CRITICAL INTEGRITY

So, Daniel had integrity, both personally and professionally. A third quality he possessed was that he maintained his integrity while under scrutiny. Daniel 6 continues,

So the governors and satraps sought to find some charge against Daniel concerning the kingdom; but they could find no charge or fault, because he was faithful; nor was there any error or fault found in him. Then these men said, "We shall not find any charge against this Daniel unless we find it against him concerning the law of his God."

So these governors and satraps thronged before the king, and said thus to him: "King Darius, live forever! All the governors of the kingdom, the administrators and satraps, the counselors and advisors, have consulted together to establish a royal statute and to make a firm decree, that whoever petitions any god or man for thirty days, except you, O king, shall be cast into the den of lions. Now, O king, establish the decree and sign the writing, so that it cannot be changed, according to the law of the Medes and Persians, which does not alter." Therefore King Darius signed the written decree. (vv. 4–9)

There were a hundred and twenty provincial rulers and three administrators in the new administration, yet the king set Daniel above all of them, putting him in charge of the whole realm of Babylon. And that's where the jealousy kicked in. A lot of the other guys may have seen this as their opportunity to jockey for position, especially now that Daniel was going to be promoted, perhaps over them. That's just straight-up envy and jealousy. Anytime you occupy a position of authority, power, or prominence, you will be eyed by the envious and exposed to criticism. It just comes with the territory. They did it to Daniel, and they'll do it to you. Paul said we should "rejoice with those who rejoice, and weep with those who weep" (Romans 12:15). Try doing that. It's a lot harder than it sounds. It's much easier to hurt with the hurting than to celebrate with those who got a huge raise when you didn't!

Daniel was promoted to be in charge over the rest of the rulers, and they thought, *No way. This has got to stop right now.* So they put him under the microscope. Their eyes became more critical than ever. Unbelievers notoriously look for some sin in Christians' lives. They're watching for some gotcha moment that, in their minds, either invalidates your Christianity or causes them to label you a hypocrite. But even under scrutiny, Daniel was blameless and above reproach. There were no skeletons lurking in his closet. Here was a powerful political figure in whom there was no corruption. Imagine that! Their investigation of Daniel's past turned up nothing. *Nada.* He was squeaky clean.

It was Lord Acton who said, "Power tends to corrupt and absolute power corrupts absolutely."[9] But here, with Daniel having almost absolute power, there was no corruption. Zilch. There was no dirt on Daniel.

I, along with most Americans, have always admired Billy Graham. Because of his international fame, he's constantly been under the media's eye of scrutiny. Yet since 1955 Graham has made George Gallup's "Ten Most Admired Men in America" list fifty-seven times![10] Even under critical close examination, Billy Graham has remained a faithful man, with a character above reproach. What you hear when he speaks is consistent with what you hear and see from him privately. And I've known others besides him who have inspired me and encouraged me to die on the right hill—to display unswerving faithfulness over the long haul. Daniel had integrity—personally, professionally, and even while under scrutiny. But there's a final "wall" that completes Daniel's city of faithful living.

THE WALL OF SPIRITUAL INTEGRITY

The story continues:

> Now when Daniel knew that the writing was signed, he went home. And in his upper room, with his windows open toward Jerusalem, he knelt down on his knees three times that day, and prayed and gave thanks before his God, as was his custom since early days.
>
> Then these men assembled and found Daniel praying and making supplication before his God. And they went before the king, and spoke concerning the king's decree: "Have you not signed a decree that every man who petitions any god or man within thirty days, except you, O king, shall be cast into the den of lions?"
>
> The king answered and said, "The thing is true,

according to the law of the Medes and Persians, which does not alter."

So they answered and said before the king, "That Daniel, who is one of the captives from Judah, does not show due regard for you, O king, or for the decree that you have signed, but makes his petition three times a day."

And the king, when he heard these words, was greatly displeased with himself, and set his heart on Daniel to deliver him; and he labored till the going down of the sun to deliver him. Then these men approached the king, and said to the king, "Know, O king, that it is the law of the Medes and Persians that no decree or statute which the king establishes may be changed." (Daniel 6:10–15)

So the government told Daniel, "You cannot pray." And Daniel responded by heading straight home to do just that. Opening his windows and facing toward Jerusalem, he prayed in hope and anticipation that one day he would return home after the captivity. And he did this on his knees three times a day. But Daniel wasn't intending to simply defy the government or to be "in your face." He was just being faithful. We know this because Daniel 6:10 reminds us that this was "his custom since early days." Daniel was doing what Daniel had always done. Nothing new or novel here. Three times a day Daniel prayed in the past, and three times a day Daniel kept doing it.

Of course, Daniel could have said, "Okay, I'll lie low for thirty days. One month can't hurt. If I do that, the statute of limitations for that law will be over, and then I can go back to my regular praying. God will understand." Or he could have said, "I'll pray, but I'll do it in private. After all, religion is a private thing." You know, separation of church and state, right? Nope. Daniel just kept on with his usual custom, opening the windows unashamedly toward Jerusalem. Had Daniel changed to do this in private instead of praying publicly as he had always done, he would have discredited his testimony and compromised his integrity and faithfulness to the Lord. His enemies, these jealous men, would have thought, *Aha, it worked! We got him to stop praying.* But Daniel believed that it's better to die for a conviction than to live with a compromise. I am filled with conviction about this verse because I think of all the lame excuses I've made for not being consistent and faithful in my prayer life: "Oh, I need my sleep, my beauty sleep. I exercise at that time. A good show is on television. I'm just so busy with work." Instead, this is a hill that Daniel was willing to die on.

God is looking for faithful men and women—followers He can depend on. I'm praying that He will find that faithful integrity in me and in you. It just takes setting your hand to the plow and plodding along, one foot in front of the other, like William Carey. Being faithful is a daily thing, an hourly thing, that ultimately becomes that one-way, lifelong obedience. One choice at a time leads to a day filled with godly choices, eventually resulting in weeks and years of God-honoring decisions that paint a picture of solid character. Consistent, righteous behavior creates a habit of integrity that will strengthen your faith.

I once heard the story of a man named George Boldt. Boldt managed a small hotel in Philadelphia, Pennsylvania. It wasn't much of a hotel, but George was a good manager and he eventually turned that twenty-four-room hotel into a great one. One evening a couple came into George's lobby and asked for a room. George said, "I'm sorry, but our rooms are filled. There's no vacancy. Not a single room here." George also knew there were no other rooms available in the city of Philadelphia. Travel was up, and visitors were flooding into the city, filling every hotel in the area. But knowing that if the couple left his hotel they wouldn't find a room, George said, "Listen, why don't you take my room? I'll sleep out on the couch tonight."

They replied, "Oh, we can't take your room." But George insisted. "If you don't take my offer, you won't find a room anywhere." So they agreed, spending the night. And as they were checking out the next morning, the visiting gentleman said to George Boldt, "You know, you are a good manager. You ought to be managing the biggest, finest hotel in the world," adding, "and I'm going to build it one day."

A few years later George received a letter in the mail from a man in New York. It was the same man who had visited that night. They had become friends during that time and the man invited George to visit him in New York for a few days. Once there, George looked up to see a big, beautiful hotel. Then his friend approached him and said, "George, I'd like you to manage this hotel."[11]

That gentleman's name was William Waldorf Astor, one of the wealthiest men in America. He had just built the Astoria Hotel, which eventually became the Waldorf Astoria, one of the finest hotels ever. Astor knew that if George Boldt could be faithful in managing a little hotel in Philadelphia and be that caring for his patrons, then he would do a great job managing the Waldorf Astoria.

What about you? How are you managing your life? Because how you're managing your life now will largely determine the position and rewards you get when you get to heaven (1 Corinthians 3:11–15; 9:24–25; Luke 19:17; 2 Timothy 4:8). We are saved by grace alone, but we are rewarded according to the integrity of our *faithfulness*. So be a faithful worker. Be a faithful husband, wife, child, and friend. Work hard. Have an excellent spirit. Every day. The martyred missionary Jim Elliot once said, "Wherever you are, *be all there*. Live to the hilt every situation you believe to be the will of God."[12]

STEPPING IT UP TO A HIGHER LEVEL

Another noteworthy and admirable quality Daniel possessed was steadfastness. Another corollary of integrity, steadfastness is a level above faithfulness. It refers to being faithful in extreme times. It's faithfulness with a shot of strength and intensity. It's faithfulness with a risk factor. Being steadfast means firmly grasping the promises of God. William Barclay writes, "So often we have a kind of vague, wistful longing that the promises of Jesus should be true. The only way really to enter into them is to believe in them with the clutching intensity of someone who is drowning."[13]

Daniel defied the earthly king because of his faithfulness to his heavenly King. Now he was facing possible death. Even so, he still believed, trusted, and clung to God's promises "with the clutching intensity of someone who is drowning." Even when life doesn't seem fair, we know God will eventually bring fairness and equity—not always immediately, but eventually. What happened to Daniel didn't seem fair—the threat of the lions' den. And he wouldn't be delivered from it; he would have to go through it before being helped.

David wrote, "Yea, though I walk *through* the valley of the shadow of death" (Psalm 23:4). Oh, how we hate when this happens. We resist walking through the valley of the shadow of death. We want to be airlifted from mountain peak to mountain peak, missing the valleys altogether. But that's not real life, is it? We need to know how to face even extreme reality in this life. And for Christians, one thing we can count on is persecution. According to Jesus, persecution is inevitable (John 15:18–20). Persecution is the world's response to God's truth. Daniel 6:5 tells us Daniel's envious accusers admitted, "We shall not find any charge against this Daniel unless we find it against him concerning the law of his God."

And so they persuaded the king to sign a thirty-day decree stating everyone in the empire was forbidden to pray to any gods except Darius (6:7). Talk about an ego! Then these men proceeded to find Daniel "praying and making supplication before his God" (6:11). The text seems to indicate that all of this took place in one day. It was a Persian custom that a death or an execution should be carried out before nightfall. The governors and satraps knew Daniel was devoted to God, and they knew Daniel's love for God would be paramount in his life, so they exploited that situation in order to get him killed.

For steadfast, committed believers, persecution is unavoidable. You and I are not going to get through this life without some battle scars. We are going to have some wounds because of opposition to our faith, and here's why: you are a part of the kingdom of light. Out there is the kingdom of darkness (your former home). When the kingdom of light and the kingdom of darkness come into contact, there's a kingdom clash. And fireworks. Paul put it this way: "All who desire to live godly in Christ Jesus will suffer persecution" (2 Timothy 3:12).

If you are steadfast in your faith, then others will definitely know you're a Christian—and not everyone will like it. They will talk behind your back. They will marginalize you. They may try to keep you from being promoted, or worse. During my years as a pastor, I've received numerous death threats, claiming,

"We're going to kill you," or "We're going to burn down your church."

NOT AN EASIER LIFE, BUT A BETTER ONE

Strangely, among some Christians there is a misconception that following Jesus Christ somehow makes life *easier*. Uh, no! Ever read the New Testament? The early church had it *anything* but easy. Even so, people make entire cottage industries of a few promises Jesus said, conveniently ignoring other promises Jesus and the Bible also make. But no one ever claims Paul's promise of persecution! Jesus told His followers, "Behold, I send you out as sheep in the midst of wolves. Therefore be wise as serpents and harmless as doves" (Matthew 10:16). Every now and then somebody will say, "Wouldn't it be great to live in the time of the apostles?" I say, "Eh, *sort of.*" Parts of it would be cool, but a whole lot of it *not so much!* In ways we can hardly imagine, the apostles were constant targets of persecution, receiving threats not only to their health, freedom, and safety but also to their integrity and character. Jesus told His disciples to expect persecution from three sources: the religious establishment, the secular world, and your own family.

THE RELIGIOUS ESTABLISHMENT

Jesus said, "Beware of men, for they will deliver you up to councils and scourge you in their synagogues" (Matthew 10:17). Did you know that organized religion has been one of the chief antagonists against the gospel? It still is today. Our church, Calvary Albuquerque, sends missionaries to many parts of the world. Our missionaries consistently tell us it's typically not the local people or government who oppose them, but rather religious organizations who try to stop their evangelistic work. And who were Jesus' worst enemies? Let's see . . . the scribes, Pharisees, Sadducees—*religious* people. Even Daniel's antagonists had a religious bent, forbidding the worship of any god *except theirs.* Somebody once defined a spiritual fanatic as somebody who loves Jesus more than you do. People from the religious establishment will be wary of fanatics like you who make too much of God.

THE SECULAR WORLD

Jesus promised, "You will be brought before governors and kings for My sake, as a testimony to them and to the Gentiles" (Matthew 10:18). A steadfast believer is sort of like a 500-watt lightbulb in a pitch-black room. It will dispel the darkness, but it will also irritate people. It irritated the Roman government when the apostles shone as bright lights for the gospel. And just as Jesus predicted, they were burned at the stake, executed, crucified, and sewn into the skins of animals so that beasts could tear them apart. The emperor Nero even set them ablaze so that they could serve as torches at night.[14] This world, with its values of darkness, hates it when we flip on the light switch.

YOUR OWN FAMILY

Jesus warned, "Now brother will deliver up brother to death, and a father his child; and children will rise up against parents and cause them to be put to death" (Matthew 10:21). There are still some cultures today where if a person converts to Christianity, a funeral is held for that family member. They will say, "He's dead to us. Don't even mention his name." Other cultures are more radical and practice "honor killings." They supposedly honor their god by killing family members who profess faith in Christ.[15] Perhaps you've discovered that witnessing to your own family members is harder than witnessing to anybody else. They laugh at you and say, "Who are you trying to kid? We grew up with you. We know you. So don't get all spiritual on us!" And that's when you learn, like Daniel, to let your life do most of the talking.

Because persecution is inevitable, trust is essential. Daniel 6:16 states, "So the king gave the command, and they brought Daniel and cast him into the den of lions." When you think of this den, think *pit*. While I was in Babylon, an archaeologist showed me a square hole on the pavement where I was standing, and underneath was a large cavern. In Daniel's day this pit would have been divided into two sections: one for the lions and one for the *hors d'oeuvre* (in this case, Daniel). Then the lions would be let loose for dinnertime. Curiously, after Daniel was thrown down into the lions' pit, this pagan king seemed to lean toward Daniel's faith, saying, "Your God, whom you serve continually, He will deliver you" (v. 16).

What on earth would prompt this godless king to say such a thing? Well, by this time Darius had been on the throne for at least a year, maybe longer. Daniel, as we already know, was old, not afraid of anybody, *and* he was on the king's council. So this king had most likely heard message after message about Daniel's life from Daniel's own lips. He heard what happened with Nebuchadnezzar and with Belshazzar. The enduring integrity of Daniel's faithfulness was well recorded in history books by that time, and Daniel had been a persistent, steadfast witness before this king.

A LIONS' DEN BECOMES A PETTING ZOO

The story continues:

> Then a stone was brought and laid on the mouth of the den, and the king sealed it with his own signet ring and with the signets of his lords, that the purpose concerning Daniel might not be changed.
>
> Now the king went to his palace and spent the night fasting; and no musicians were brought before him. Also his sleep went from him. (Daniel 6:17–18)

I find it amazing that a pagan king was losing sleep over this godly old man, Daniel. Oh, and by the way, nowhere did Daniel complain or say, "This isn't fair! God, I've served You seventy years. I deserve better!" In fact, we don't have a record of Daniel saying anything at all. Daniel knew his death was imminent. But like Jesus, he "opened not [h]is mouth" (Isaiah 53:7) and instead was silent before his antagonists as he was lowered into a den of hungry lions. Think of the faith it took for Daniel to remain calm in the face of such circumstances.

Centuries later, in AD 156, another God-follower by the name of Polycarp, a Christian leader and bishop in Smyrna, was brought to be burned at the stake. Once there, they tied him up and lit the fire. The executioner offered him a way out, saying, "Polycarp, you can get out of this if you want. Just deny Jesus, and we'll let you go and you'll have your freedom." But Polycarp confidently declared, "Eighty and six years have I served him [about the same age as Daniel], and he never once wronged me; how then shall I blaspheme my King, Who hath saved me?"[16] Polycarp accepted those flames as the will of God for his life.

I believe Daniel similarly saw the lions' den but didn't squawk. He was steadfast enough to know and believe, *Okay, this is it. I've served God for eighty years; now it's the lions' den for me.* Obviously, it's easy to talk about suffering, but this is where that clutching intensity of a drowning man has to kick in. This is where the steadfastness of your integrity is shown to be real. In Psalm 51:10, David prayed, "Create in me a clean heart, O God, and renew a *steadfast* spirit within me." The Hebrew word translated "steadfast" in that verse means to be fixed or fastened, immovable. Psalm 112:7 describes a godly man, saying, "He will not be afraid of evil tidings; his heart is *steadfast*, trusting in the LORD."

So what would it take to shake your faith? To rattle your resolve? To persuade you to fall away from following God? What would it take to convince you to stop trusting Jesus Christ? The death of a child? A lingering disease? Loss of employment? Disappointment or betrayal by your church or other believers? What would cause you to declare, "I can no longer follow a God who would let this happen"?

Some years ago, I had a conversation with a young lady who confessed, "Well, I used to believe in Jesus. I followed and trusted Him. But then my grandmother died, and that was it." I said, "I'm sorry for your loss; that is very painful. But I have to ask, did you really think your grandmother was never going to die? Because that's never happened before in history. If it was your grandmother's death that caused you to decide, 'I'm not following Jesus anymore,' you set a pretty unrealistic expectation for belief."

Remember Job? He lost his estate, all ten of his children, and his health, yet he concluded, "The LORD gave, and the LORD has taken away; blessed be the name of the LORD" (Job 1:21). And when his situation got even worse, he said, "Though He slay me, yet will I trust Him" (Job 13:15). In other words, "God can kill me, but I'm not going to be moved."

That's steadfastness.

Woodland Christian Church in Kansas City, Missouri, once

adopted this as their slogan: "Wake up, sing up, pray up, and pay up, but never give up, or let up, or back up, or shut up, until the kingdom of Christ is built up in this world." Pretty good, huh?

So back to King Darius. Following a sleepless night in Babylon, he got up at sunrise and hurried over to the lion pit. He yelled down into the pit, "Daniel, servant of the living God" (Daniel 6:20). *What?* Why did he call him that? Because he had watched Daniel. He'd seen Daniel live out a steadfast faith, so much so that even this pagan ruler suspected all the gods of Babylon and Medo-Persia were fake. They were just a bunch of statues without life. They were dead deities, far different from the living God. Daniel's integrity convicted him. So the king declared that truth and asked, "Has your God, whom you serve continually, been able to deliver you from the lions?"

If this were a movie, there would be a dramatic pause here as the camera slowly moves from the daylight outside into the darkness of that den. Then Daniel would step into the ray of light coming through the open hatch in the ceiling. That's when he would speak these words:

O king, live forever! My God sent His angel and shut the lions' mouths, so that they have not hurt me, because I was found innocent before Him; and also, O king, I have done no wrong before you. (Daniel 6:21–22)

Then notice King Darius's response:

> Now the king was exceedingly glad for him, and commanded that they should take Daniel up out of the den. So Daniel was taken up out of the den, and no injury whatever was found on him, *because he believed in his God.*
>
> And the king gave the command, and they brought those men who had accused Daniel, and they cast them into the den of lions—them, their children, and their wives; and the lions overpowered them, and broke all their bones in pieces before they ever came to the bottom of the den. (Daniel 6:23–24)

Every kid knows this story. Every Sunday school relentlessly recounts it. Daniel was delivered from the lions' mouths. And though it doesn't always happen this way, when it does, it's pretty marvelous, isn't it?

Radio legend Paul Harvey once told a story about West Side Baptist Church in Beatrice, Nebraska. This church held choir practice every Wednesday evening, without fail. Most choir members would arrive early at 7:15 p.m., just so they could be sure to start on time. But on one particular Wednesday night, for various reasons, the choir members were late. The piano player had taken an afternoon nap and slept too long. A student had homework problems, so she came late. Several of the members' cars wouldn't start, causing them to be late. In fact, every single choir member failed to show up, and so not one of them was at the church on time. And it turned out to be a good thing, because on that particular day there was an undetected gas leak in the basement. At precisely 7:25 p.m., that gas leak ignited the furnace and the entire church blew up! The explosion would have surely killed or seriously injured everyone in that choir. But nobody was there.[17]

I love stories like that, and they do happen—but not always. Even if you love and believe in God like Daniel did, they don't always happen. Isaiah believed and was sawn in half. Peter believed and was crucified upside down. Paul believed and was delivered a number of times, but then a Roman axe severed his head from his body. Daniel thought, *This is either going to be a wonderful rescue, or I'll see You in a few, Lord.*

Either way it would have been deliverance! Daniel either would have been looking into the face of God or the face of Darius, saying, "O king, live forever!" Deliverance is possible, but not always promised.

The best part of this story is the lingering influence that Daniel imprinted on this ruler's life:

Then king Darius wrote:
    To all peoples, nations, languages that dwell in all
        the earth:

Peace be multiplied to you.

I make a decree that in every dominion of my kingdom men must tremble and fear before the God
of Daniel.

For He is the living God,
And steadfast forever;
His kingdom is the one which shall not be destroyed,
And His dominion shall endure to the end.
He delivers and rescues,
And He works signs and wonders
In heaven and on earth,
Who has delivered Daniel from the power of the
lions.

So this Daniel prospered in the reign of Darius and in
the reign of Cyrus the Persian. (Daniel 6:25–28)

Daniel. One guy who influenced two empires. In the
Babylonian Empire, Daniel influenced Nebuchadnezzar and
Belshazzar, and here he made a lasting impression on Darius the
Mede in the Medo-Persian Empire. But as we saw in chapter 1,
Daniel's influence likely extended beyond that. The Babylonian
word for "wise men" in the book of Daniel is *Magi*. So what
were Magi from Babylon doing showing up after Christ was
born looking for the King of the Jews? Bible scholars believe

Daniel's book may have tipped off the Magi to the future King, and they took the tip and the trip, eventually showing up at Mary and Joseph's house. That's pretty impressive.

See, it doesn't take *a lot* of people to change a culture; it just takes the *right* people. If one or two who are steadfast in their God can influence a nation, then they can surely influence a family. Never underestimate the power of a godly life. There's something about being around a righteous, godly man or woman that can be very contagious. After all, isn't that what you want to become? Don't you want to stand up for your God? Don't you want to influence people for Him? Is that in your heart to do? If so, then these words are for you: "Therefore, my beloved brethren, be steadfast, immovable, always abounding in the work of the Lord, knowing that your labor is not in vain in the Lord" (1 Corinthians 15:58). That's a great biblical definition of *integrity*.

> It doesn't take *a lot* of people to change a culture; it just takes the *right* people.

Former US Senate chaplain Peter Marshall told a story called "The Keeper of the Spring." He said there was an Austrian village that had a beautiful stream running through it. This village was surrounded by the Alps. And they hired this guy called the Keeper of the Spring to patrol the hills and to collect debris from the pools that fed the stream that ran through the town. He picked up leaves and branches and anything that would pollute or contaminate that stream in the village. And because he did such a faithful job with quiet regularity patrolling those hills, the stream that ran through that village was beautiful, clear, and pristine. Swans and tourists came, businesses built their shops there, and farmlands were irrigated.

One day the village elders had a meeting and were looking at the budget. One of the elders said, "What is this line item for a salary we're paying some guy called the Keeper of the Spring? I've never seen this person, have you?" None of them had ever seen him before. They said, "Yeah, but people say he's up there and he's working, and you can't see him, but that's why everything is so nice here in town." The village elder said, "I think it's a scam." And so they took a vote and fired the Keeper of the Spring.

For a while, nothing changed in town; everything was exactly the same. But after a few weeks, summer turned to fall, the leaves started dropping, the twigs on the trees started breaking off, and the debris started mounting up and clogging the stream. It was then that the villagers noticed the stream wasn't so clear anymore. It had a yellow tint, a few days later it was brownish, and soon a stench came from it. Then the swans left . . . along with the tourists. The water wheels that diverted the water from the stream into the fields to be irrigated slowed down and eventually stopped. The village elders realized their error and said, "Go get that guy and hire him back." So they found the Keeper of the Spring and gave him his job back, and within weeks the water was restored to its pristine beauty.[18]

Peter Marshall's point was that what the Keeper of the Spring was to that Austrian village, the steadfast believer is to the world. One life well lived can impact a family, a neighborhood, a city, a country . . . or two nations!

Daniel was a "keeper of the spring." And so are you. Jesus had twelve disciples, and He told them, "Go." Within a single generation the entire known world had heard the gospel. That's steadfastness.

You and I need to find a hill worth dying on. And we need to decide where the line in the sand will be drawn, where our devotion to Christ will supersede our conformity to any other standard. The higher you aim, the greater your influence will be. You may be scorned for it, resisted because of it, and even lose your life over it. But know this—you're keeping the spring flowing. You're influencing lots of people downstream who need the beauty and refreshment of your commitment to Jesus Christ.

But you can't be a keeper of the spring until you've tasted and drunk from that stream of Living Water yourself. That's where you begin. That's where you discover that your faith in Jesus is the hill worth dying on. And that's when you achieve real life purpose, meaning, and direction. You want a cause to live for? Then sell yourself out for a steadfast devotion to Jesus Christ.

And do it today.

DARE TO DEFY NORMAL: INTEGRITY

Integrity is moral uprightness and consistency. Your words match your deeds, and your character is the same whether anyone is watching or not. Daniel's integrity sustained him before God and men. Those who tried to bring him down couldn't do so, because Daniel kept his focus on doing what was right before God. It wasn't about perfection but consistency—good character over time. With that in mind, I dare you to take a hard look at your integrity.

How do the four walls of integrity look in your life?

PERSONAL

- *Deliberate*: While you as a believer are saved by grace, you are rewarded according to your faithfulness. The whole idea of following Jesus is based on the idea that God wants a real relationship with you, not just religious actions and attitudes.

- *Defy Normal*: Real relationships require integrity, and that always begins with a good, hard look at yourself. First, answer these questions from other people's point of view—your spouse, your boss or coworker, your friends, your fellow Christians. You can ask those people these questions if you want to. Then answer them for yourself.

  ¤ What word(s) describe your character?

    ☐   What song would be your life's soundtrack? Why?

    ☐   What would be your life's motto? Why?

Do you see any discrepancies? Anything you want to change about yourself? Identify those things, and then ask God to help you to develop (or maintain) integrity in your life.

PROFESSIONAL

- *Deliberate*: Integrity will put you in the spotlight at work—not only to receive praise but also to be closely scrutinized. If you are in the habit of working hard and having a good attitude, people are going to notice. That may open doors for you to share what you believe. It may also open up opportunities for you to do more because you've been faithful in what you've done already. Are you known first for being a great worker and doing quality work, or for being "that Christian who's always at odds with someone or something"?

- *Defy Normal*: Read Colossians 3:23, Ephesians 5:5–9, and Ecclesiastes 5:18–20. Then respond to the following questions with total honesty:

  ☐   How much does excellence in your work matter to you? How much does it matter to God?

  ☐   If you are a boss, are you worth following?

  ☐   If you're a worker, are you dependable, reliable, and trustworthy?

CRITICAL

- *Deliberate*: Can your life stand up to scrutiny? How do you respond to people who criticize or challenge you in matters of character? You don't have to pretend that everyone is your friend. Jesus doesn't call you to do that, but He does call you to respond to your enemies with love, not bitterness or anger.

- *Defy Normal*: Skeptic-proof your life. Take a look at your work habits, how you spend your free time, and your ability to weep and rejoice with others. Write down three things you're doing that honor God in those areas, and three things you need to work on. When you pray, thank God for the progress you've made in honoring Him and ask Him to help with the things you need to work on.

SPIRITUAL

- *Deliberate*: Consistency with God will lead to consistency in other areas of your life. The more you follow God, the more His character will rub off on you.

- *Defy Normal*: Read the Bible each day for the next twenty-one days. If you're not sure where to start, try the gospel of John, Psalms, or Proverbs. It doesn't matter whether it's five minutes or thirty, but start each time by asking God to show you something in His Word. When

He does, write it down. At the end of the three weeks, read through what you've recorded.

☐ What did you learn about God?

☐ What did you learn about yourself?

☐ How can these things help you develop or maintain integrity—consistently upright, moral behavior?

CHAPTER FIVE

RISE ABOVE

DEPENDENCE

The words *prayer* and *controversial* don't seem to go together. They don't even belong in the same sentence, mainly due to the fact that there's nothing controversial about prayer, right?

Wrong.

Instead of being welcomed, encouraged, and revered, prayer in postmodern America is now considered by many to be offensive, revolting, and even un-American. Sounds crazy, doesn't it? I mean, wasn't prayer one of the foundation stones of our nation? True, and yet it seems history is now repeating itself, because prayer was controversial just prior to the Revolutionary War that birthed our country. One of the reasons we are a nation is that we rebelled against a tyrannical government that sought to curtail our freedom to worship and to pray according to the dictates of our own heart. So we revolted against that oppression, forming our very own "nation under God." Now, around 240 years later, prayer is back in the spotlight—and not in a positive way. More specifically, the real controversy lies in the use of a certain name in prayer.

In many situations, prayer is considered harmless and innocuous. But the mere mention of one particular name suddenly sends shockwaves of offense, opposition, and protest reverberating through our nation. No one bats an eye if you pray to Mother Earth, Father Time, or some other fictitious, generic deity. But the moment you mention the name Jesus Christ, people cringe and cry foul, throwing fits and tantrums of politically correct protests. When my friend Franklin Graham prayed at the 2001 presidential inauguration, he closed the prayer, predictably, in the strong name of Jesus Christ. And as expected, people were upset. "How dare he pray in the name of Jesus," they complained. One atheist went so far as to file a lawsuit against the government for allowing the prayer to be spoken.[1] Really?

That's the kind of public furor I'm talking about. Mentioning the name of Jesus to unbelievers and some religious types is like holding up a crucifix to a vampire in some campy 1960s horror flick. It causes them to recoil in disgust. They hate it. And they want it immediately removed.

According to *U.S. News and World Report*, the current White House is insisting that all public rallies on a national level, including those that involve prayer, must first be approved, commissioned, and vetted by the White House itself.[2] In other words, they must be preapproved and edited by the state. Brilliant. So now the government wants to tell us *how* and how *not* to pray. This type of control and censorship sounds an awful lot like the country we rebelled against 240 years ago—or maybe even worse. So it seems we've come full circle. We have become what we once hated. Not long ago, I saw a *Washington Post* article about a high school graduation where a student offered a public prayer. And as expected, it drew criticism. An atheist student—who incidentally had walked off having anticipated the prayer—was very upset. Only a minute and a half long, the prayer really wasn't that controversial. In fact, it was very benign, and didn't even include the name of Jesus. However, that didn't stop an atheist group from accusing the student who prayed of "inflict[ing] Christian prayer on a captive audience."[3]

How could prayer—something so holy and righteous—come to be considered so unpopular and evil?

Our friend Daniel faced similar controversial circumstances. In fact, as you remember from reading chapter 4 of this book, the whole reason Daniel was put in the lions' den was because of prayer. Daniel's contemporaries had tricked King Darius into passing a law that stated no one could pray to any god other than the king. But Daniel continued to open his windows toward Jerusalem to pray, and he got thrown in the lions' den for it.

Have you ever wondered, from a spiritual level, why prayer to our God is so controversial? I suspect part of the reason has something to do with the fact that Satan knows prayer is a powerful force. He is well aware that prayer, if engaged in regularly, spells his demise, his defeat, and the thwarting of his influence in your life. So it makes perfect sense that he would do anything he can to keep you from it.

Our problem is we typically resort to prayer only when the bombs are falling and a crisis is happening. Prayer often becomes like pulling a fire alarm or dialing 911. Or we use prayer like the tomato frog of Madagascar uses its poison. When attacked by a predator the tomato frog exudes a milky, white poison all over its skin so that when the predator gets the frog in its mouth and tastes the poison, it spits the frog out. But by that time the damage has already been done to the frog, and typically it dies from the attack. It's a case of "too little, too late."

We often pray like that—*after* Satan has attacked and the damage is already done. Daniel, however, was a "proactive pray-er" and one of the greatest Old Testament models of what true, effective communication with God is all about. Of course, the greatest model prayer in the entire Bible is what Jesus taught His disciples to pray: "Our Father in heaven, hallowed be Your name. Your kingdom come. Your will be done on earth as it is in heaven" (Matthew 6:9–10).

FOUR "STRANDS" IN THE ROPE OF PRAYER

Interestingly, we find many similarities between Daniel's prayer and the one Jesus taught us to pray. Daniel's was a prayer with balance. It wasn't all petition: "I need, I want, give me, help me." But it also wasn't all praise either. Rather, it involved four characteristics that beautifully complement one another.

Charles Haddon Spurgeon once said, "Prayer pulls the rope down below and the great bell rings above in the ears of God."[4] With that in mind, I want to give you four "strands" of the rope that rings that bell in God's ears.

Daniel 9:4–19 records Daniel's prayer. I've included it here in its entirety because I want you to experience the depth of Daniel's devotion to his God in prayer. Here it is beginning in verse 3:

> Then I set my face toward the Lord God to make request by prayer and supplications, with fasting, sackcloth, and ashes. And I prayed to the LORD my God, and made confession, and said, "O Lord, great and awesome God, who keeps His covenant and mercy with those who love Him, and with those who keep His commandments, we have sinned and committed iniquity, we have done wickedly and rebelled, even by departing from Your precepts and Your judgments. Neither have we heeded Your servants the prophets, who spoke in Your name to our kings and our princes, to our fathers and all the people of the land. O Lord, righteousness belongs to You, but to us shame of face, as it is this day—to the men of Judah, to the inhabitants

of Jerusalem and all Israel, those near and those far off in all the countries to which You have driven them, because of the unfaithfulness which they have committed against You.

"O Lord, to us belongs shame of face, to our kings, our princes, and our fathers, because we have sinned against You. To the Lord our God belong mercy and forgiveness, though we have rebelled against Him. We have not obeyed the voice of the LORD our God, to walk in His laws, which He set before us by His servants the prophets. Yes, all Israel has transgressed Your law, and has departed so as not to obey Your voice; therefore the curse and the oath written in the Law of Moses the servant of God have been poured out on us, because we have sinned against Him. And He has confirmed His words, which He spoke against us and against our judges who judged us, by bringing upon us a great disaster; for under the whole heaven such has never been done as what has been done to Jerusalem.

"As it is written in the Law of Moses, all this disaster has come upon us; yet we have not made our prayer before the LORD our God, that we might turn from our iniquities and understand Your truth. Therefore the LORD has kept the disaster in mind, and brought it upon us; for the LORD our God is righteous in all the works which He does, though we have not obeyed His voice. And now, O Lord our God, who brought Your people out of the land of Egypt with a mighty hand, and made Yourself a name, as it is this day—we have sinned, we have done wickedly!

"O Lord, according to all Your righteousness, I pray, let Your anger and Your fury be turned away from Your city Jerusalem, Your holy mountain; because for our sins, and for the iniquities of our fathers, Jerusalem and Your people are a reproach to all those around us. Now therefore, our God, hear the prayer of Your servant, and his supplications, and for the Lord's sake cause Your face to shine on Your sanctuary, which is desolate. O my God, incline Your ear and hear; open Your eyes and see our desolations, and the city which is called by Your name; for we do not present our supplications before You because of our righteous deeds, but because of Your great mercies. O Lord, hear! O Lord, forgive! O Lord, listen and act! Do not delay for Your own sake, my God, for Your city and Your people are called by Your name." (Daniel 9:3–19)

Wow. What kind of person prays like that? In what is largely a shallow Christian culture, it's both refreshing and challenging to read of Daniel baring his heart and soul to God. And as we do, four distinguishing characteristics stand out, four "strands" in the rope of prayer.

STRAND #1: HUMBLE ADORATION

Daniel said, "I prayed to the LORD my God" (v. 4). Daniel began by recognizing to whom he was talking. He was not speaking to a friend, having a conversation with a colleague, or addressing King Darius. He was speaking to the King of kings.

I believe it's important when we pray to recognize, "I'm actually saying this to God." You may think, *Isn't that obvious? Isn't prayer, by definition, talking to God?* Yes, but believe it or not, it's possible to pray and not really talk to God, but rather to yourself and others. Have you ever prayed aloud in a group and then thought, *How did my prayer sound? Was that a good one? I sure hope they like what I just said and agree with it.*

In the gospel of Luke, Jesus told a parable about prayer. "Two men went up to the temple to pray, one a Pharisee and the other a tax collector. The Pharisee stood and prayed thus *with himself,* 'God, I thank You that I am not like other men—extortioners, unjust, adulterers, or even as this tax collector'" (Luke 18:10–11). He prayed that out loud, but he was actually praying to *himself.* This guy liked the sound of his own voice. R. A. Torrey wrote, "We should never utter one syllable of prayer, either in public or in private, until we are definitely conscious that we have come into the presence of God and are actually praying to Him."[5] And here's why this is so important. Recognizing you're talking to God gives you a needed perspective. We often bring God our problems with an attitude that says, "Lord, this is really hard. I know this sounds impossible . . ." Wait, what? That's the wrong perspective. You're talking to Someone who doesn't have the word *impossible* in His vocabulary. Because we are weak, shortsighted, and finite, we often see only our problems instead of God's power. Instead of having faith in God's ability, we become fixated on our inability. The problem is so close and looms large—all the while our view of God grows smaller and smaller. But when, like Daniel, we say, "O Lord, *You are God*" from the heart, our problems are put into the right perspective, and we see them in the light of who He is.

In Acts 4, Jewish leaders forbade the early church from speaking anymore in the name of Jesus. And from a human perspective, it looked like the Jesus movement might be shut down . . . that is, until his disciples prayed. And this is what they said: "Lord, You are God, who made heaven and earth and the sea, and all that is in them" (v. 24). Now why would they bother with all of that in their prayer? I believe it's because they wanted to see their situation in the right perspective: "We're talking to the Creator, the all-powerful One here!" This helped them see the problem in light of the majesty of a big God. "Big Problem, Little Us," or "Big Problem, Bigger God!" It's a huge contrast in perspectives. This is why Jews typically begin their prayers like this: "*Barukh atah, Adonai Eloheinu, Melekh ha'olam*"—which means, "Blessed are You, Lord our God, King of the universe."

And that's exactly who we're talking to—*the* King of the universe. Doesn't that fire you up? We have this kind of access to the One who spoke the galaxies into existence. What an honor! What a privilege! And that was Daniel's approach to prayer. He opened his prayer with, "O Lord, great and awesome God" (9:4). That's *humble adoration*—recognizing God is great in magnitude and importance.

Continuing his prayer, Daniel said, "O Lord, righteousness belongs to You" (9:7). In other words, God always does what is right, and He never makes a mistake. No fumbles. No gaffes. No oversights. You never have to worry if He's blown it or done something wrong. He's always right. A few verses later Daniel said, "To the Lord our God belong mercy and forgiveness" (9:9). In verse 15 Daniel said God has made a name for Himself. It's not that God gets any bigger or greater than He already is, but our view of Him expands. When we recognize God's awesome power, our understanding of His greatness grows. And that fuels our faith, enabling us to survive life's issues and seemingly insurmountable problems.

> When we recognize God's awesome power, our understanding of His greatness grows.

So when Daniel prayed, he used terms that honor God's character and name. That's like praying, "Hallowed be Your name" (Matthew 6:9). If we were to contemplate our prayers, we would likely find that we spend too little time in adoration. So much of our prayers are self-focused. But adoration forces your eyes above the horizon of human difficulties and your own issues, giving you a clear and right perspective.

There's a huge difference between the emergency prayer of "Oh God!" and the adoration prayer of "O, God!" Though both involve desperation, one is a cry for help while the other is a declaration of praise.

For other people, prayer is sort of like a first-class hotel. They believe in a theology that says, "I can name it, and I can claim it. I can tell God to do this, by commanding God's power with my words." To them, God is like a celestial bellhop in a hotel—just call room service, and He will deliver.

That was not Daniel's approach at all. His prayer began not with demands but rather with humble adoration. And the more we grow in our knowledge of who God is, the more time we will spend admiring, adoring, and worshipping Him. Adoration in prayer is a mark of a maturing believer. As you and I mature, we become more aware of the fact that we are in God's presence. And that realization humbles us to the point where we cannot help but adore Him.

I once heard that the great evangelist Dwight L. Moody was busy preparing for a speaking tour. While he was in his study preoccupied with his books and upcoming messages, his eight-year-old son walked in. Moody asked, "What do you want, son?" The little boy replied, "I don't want anything, Daddy, I just want to be where you are."[6]

That's where we want to be in our lives. To be in that place where we say, "Lord, I just want to be where You are. You are great. You are awesome. I'm talking to You. I'm hanging with You." So humble adoration is the first strand in the rope of prayer.

STRAND #2: HONEST CONFESSION

Daniel had a firm grip on the "confession" strand of the prayer rope, since the longest section of his recorded prayer involves transparent confession before God. Daniel was basically saying, "We've blown it. I'm sorry. We've done this and we own up to it. We've acted wickedly." Over and over again he went through the history of the nation of Israel from the times of the kings and the prophets, showing how they repeatedly disobeyed God's voice. It's been said that the six most important words in human relationships are *I admit that I was wrong*.

These words are the most important, but they're also the hardest to say. Yet Daniel said them to God freely and repeatedly. Jesus taught His disciples to pray the same thing: "Forgive us our debts, as we forgive our debtors" (Matthew 6:12). Notice that Jesus used the plural, not the singular. Instead of saying, "*My* Father in heaven. Forgive *me*. Give *me* this day *my* daily bread," Jesus' model prayer was "us," "we," and "our." That's because He wants us to realize we are part of something bigger than just an individual. As believers, you and I are inseparably connected to one another in the local and global community of faith.

That's precisely how Daniel prayed here. In his prayer he used the word "we" fourteen times. Twenty times he used the word "our," and ten times the word "us." A total of *forty-four* times these collective pronouns were used. This attitude reveals that Daniel, though a prophet, wasn't aloof from his people. In his perspective, it wasn't "you and them" who have sinned, but rather "we and us." He was saying, "I'm a part of the problem, God. Forgive *us*, collectively." Daniel didn't point his finger at sinners. He locked arms with them, held hands with them, and said, "I'm in this with you, guys. I'm a part of this." And note that Daniel's confession naturally followed his adoration. I believe the closer you get to God, the more you become aware of your own sin, selfishness, and your need to clear the slate with God. One always follows the other. It's like singing off-key while sitting next to someone who is singing pitch-perfect. That person's perfection reveals your own imperfection.

Leonard Ravenhill said, "The self-sufficient do not need to pray; the self-satisfied will not pray; the self-righteousness *cannot* pray."[7] But those who adore God see themselves for who they really are: sinners in need of God's forgiveness. That's why we "confess" our sins, meaning we agree with God concerning our sin. And Daniel did that.

Then he went even further with this admission of guilt, using the word "shame" (9:7–8). "O Lord, righteousness belongs to You, but to us *shame* of face." This is a word of conscience—healthy humiliation, embarrassment, and guilt. Today, society says guilt is bad and that you should never feel it. Guilt is considered by many to be passé, puritanical, cruel, even damaging to the human psyche. "Get rid of guilt. You shouldn't ever live under guilt."

Years ago, a popular frozen yogurt store's advertising slogan was "All of the pleasure, none of the guilt."[7] It was a cleverly devised campaign, as they knew people in this culture want to banish guilt altogether. But here's what we have to understand. There's bad guilt and there's good guilt. Bad guilt is when a person just feels guilty about everything. This usually stems from a sense of insecurity. But then there's also good guilt, which is what emotionally healthy people feel when they actually *are* guilty!

When a person is guilty, he or she ought to feel guilty. That's healthy. The reason for this is that good guilt is either from the Holy Spirit or your conscience. Either way, it drives you to the Savior to get it taken care of, and that's always a good thing. So Daniel prayed by looking upward (adoration) and then by looking inward (confession).

STRAND #3: HEARTFELT PETITION

Now Daniel looked *outward.* He prayed for what he saw happening around him:

> O Lord, according to all Your righteousness, I pray, let Your anger and Your fury be turned away from Your city Jerusalem, Your holy mountain; because for our sins, and for the iniquities of our fathers, Jerusalem and Your

people are a reproach to all those around us. Now therefore, our God, hear the prayer of Your servant, and his
supplications, and for the Lord's sake cause Your face to
shine on Your sanctuary, which is desolate. O my God,
incline Your ear and hear; open Your eyes and see our
desolations, and the city which is called by Your name;
for we do not present our supplications before You because of our righteous deeds, but because of Your great
mercies. (Daniel 9:16–18)

Then he concluded, "O Lord, hear! O Lord, forgive! O
Lord, listen and act! Do not delay for Your own sake, my God,
for Your city and Your people are called by Your name" (Daniel
9:19).

This is really the only time in this prayer Daniel actually
asked God for something, and his request was very specific. "O
Lord, You see it—now do something. Listen, look, act, *do it!*"
By the way, that was Daniel's version of "amen."[8]

Daniel had read in Jeremiah's prophecy that after seventy
years God was going to bring Israel back to Jerusalem (Jeremiah
29:10). He just wanted God to do what God said He would
do, to fulfill His promise to His people. Honestly, that's what
prayer is—prayer isn't getting things *from* God as much as getting *in* on things *with* God, to remind God of His pledge to His
beloved. "Lord, You said You're going to do it. I believe You're
going to do it. Do it!" I fear that sometimes our prayers are weak

and vague, like "Lord, just bless everyone, everywhere, with everything. Amen." Or, have you ever heard this one? "Lord, You know every request spoken and unspoken." Seriously? When I hear that, I always think, *Okay, but since you're already praying, why don't you just go ahead and tell God what that is, specifically?* If you walked into a restaurant and said, "I have an unspoken food need. Bless me," they'd look at you like you're the weirdest person on earth.

God wants us to be specific in our prayers, just like Daniel was. But Daniel's petition was also sympathetic in that he focused his prayer on others. Daniel wasn't in Jerusalem at the time, so he was praying for that city from afar. In fact, Daniel would never return to Jerusalem; he would spend the rest of his days in Babylon. But other Jews *would* be returning, so he prayed for them.

Scripture calls this kind of praying *intercessory prayer*. It's the hardest type of praying because you're asking on behalf of others instead of yourself. Think about it. Worship is easier than intercession because God is so amazing. He gives awesome blessings, is infinitely powerful, and knows everything. So worship is very natural for a child of God. I mean, it would be awfully narcissistic not to engage in worship. And I find that praying for myself is also pretty easy, even if it's confession. I am well aware of what I've done wrong. And I know what I want, so that's relatively easy to do. But when I start praying for other people, that's *labor*, and that's also usually when I get a bad case of spiritual ADD. That's when my passion for prayer can start to fade. Can you identify? It's during this kind of praying when you start falling asleep or become distracted by a million other things. The reason for this is because you're not as emotionally in touch with other people's needs as you are your own. It really makes you admire a guy like Epaphras, whom Paul described as "a bondservant of Christ . . . always laboring fervently for you in prayers" (Colossians 4:12).

By the way, if anyone ever talks to God on your behalf, thank them and consider yourself blessed. Just to know that someone took the time to unselfishly pray for you is a huge thing. And it inspires you to do the same for someone else.

Intercession is hard work, but it is necessary. If you don't include intercession in your prayer life, you will eventually become more and more self-absorbed, just another spiritual couch potato—consuming, feeding yourself, and becoming a lifetime member of the International "Bless Me" Club. And your prayers will basically be reduced to "Well, here I am, God. Bless me now and give me stuff." For people like this, life is all about *intake* and what makes them feel good. Because there are no outlets to give to others (especially in prayer) they become spiritually obese. The only outlet they have is to gossip, slander, or complain.

But do you know what the remedy for this is . . . *besides* repentance? Whether by pencil and paper or on your smartphone, jot down the needs of people you know. Keep a running list, and faithfully pray for them. Again, that's how Jesus also taught us to pray: "Give *us* this day *our* daily bread" (Matthew 6:11).

STRAND #4: HOLY MOTIVATION

Motivation is the fourth and final strand on the prayer rope that rings the bell that gets God's attention. There's something in the last section of Daniel's prayer I want you to notice. He said,

> Now therefore, our God, hear the prayer of Your servant, and his supplications, and *for the Lord's sake* cause Your face to shine on Your sanctuary, which is desolate. . . . O Lord, hear! O Lord, forgive! O Lord, listen and act! Do not delay for *Your* own sake, my God, for *Your* city and *Your* people are called by *Your* name. (Daniel 9:17, 19)

In Daniel's prayer, he emphasized God's glory. Over and over again, he prayed, "Your . . . Your . . . Your . . . Your." "Lord, do this for *Your* sake. We are *Your* people called by *Your* name. Do it for the sake of *Your* reputation"—that was Daniel's ultimate motivation. Daniel's motive in seeing this prayer answered was not just for the good of God's people but for the glory of God.

Incidentally, one of the reasons the New Testament says our prayers seem so ineffective or unanswered is because we pray with the wrong motives. Don't get me wrong. I think you can pray about anything in the world, but sometimes there's a fine line between our needs and our "greeds." We don't always pray with the right motives. Like Paul said, we don't always pray "as we ought" (Romans 8:26). We can spend a lot of time asking for stuff we don't need. We pray, "Lord, give me this, give me that." What would happen if we started weighing our requests by the motivation of: "Does this further the program of God in this world?" or "How does my request bring more glory to God?" How would that change the way we pray?

James, the brother of Jesus, wrote,

> You want what you don't have, so you scheme and kill to get it. You are jealous of what others have, but you can't get it, so you fight and wage war to take it away from them. Yet you don't have what you want because you don't ask God for it. And even when you ask, you don't get it because your motives are all wrong—you want only what will give you pleasure. (James 4:2–3 NLT)

The highest and most effective prayer has God's interests in mind—His fame, His glory. That should be our ultimate goal and motivation when we pray. And though we may nod in agreement at this point, is it at the very heart of why we pray? That's a convicting thought, isn't it?

So Daniel looked upward in adoration, inward in confession, outward with petition, and then he closed his prayer by looking upward again in motivation.

Daniel's prayer came full circle. Four strands formed a strong rope of prayer. Daniel initiated his prayer with adoration, and he ended it in giving God glory. That was also how Jesus taught us to pray at the end of the Lord's Prayer: "For Yours is the kingdom and the power and the glory forever. Amen" (Matthew 6:13). That's the pattern.

PULL THE ROPE

So, Christian, here is what God is saying to you about prayer: *Pull the rope. Pull it frequently and faithfully.*

Pulling the rope of prayer is one of the most basic things about the Christian life. It's like breathing. When a baby is born, the earth's atmosphere puts pressure on his lungs, and that pressure causes that baby to breathe. It forces the lungs to take in air.

When you are born into the family of God, you're born again. As a child of God you enter into the atmosphere of God's world, the spiritual sphere of His reality. The atmosphere of God's presence and grace exerts pressure on your life, and the response is prayer. It's as natural as breathing. It's probably better to say it's *super*natural. But it's not normal. That is, the world around you finds prayer strange and out of place.

The customary standard is to relegate prayer to something to be done on a periodic basis, such as at weddings and funerals. That means when your life is engaged in prayer, you immediately rise above the status quo and enter into the presence of God.

If Spurgeon was right when he said that prayer pulls the rope down below and the great bell rings above in the ears of God, then we should strive to be great bell ringers! This four-stranded rope of adoration, confession, petition, and holy motivation is our hotwire connection to God. It's where our heart pours itself out and where the blessings pour back into us.

Don't be that Christian who prays only when he or she is in a tough spot or needs a miracle. Instead, know that prayer is the pathway to a wonderful, supernatural, ongoing relationship with God. It's the kind of relationship that often prompts you to think, *Lord, I really don't want anything; I just want to be here with You. I'm not really looking for things as much as looking for what You are doing, and I want to be part of it. I just want to come along and find out what You are doing, and I want to do it with You, for You, and for Your name's sake!*

Whether that Christian's prayers are viewed as controversial or not, the person who learns to pray this way will be, like Daniel, someone who overcomes difficult

> Prayer is the pathway to a wonderful, supernatural, ongoing relationship with God.

circumstances. Defying normal, they will be lifted beyond life's gravity, no matter how strong, "because He who is in you is greater than he who is in the world" (1 John 4:4).

DARE TO DEFY NORMAL: DEPENDENCE

Prayer is the Christian's secret weapon—partly in the cool, ace-up-the-sleeve way, but also in the gathering-dust-on-the-shelf sense. Too many believers neglect the unique access to God that Jesus purchased for us on the cross. If you belong to Christ, you have personal, one-on-one access to the Creator of the universe—and what's more, you can call Him *Dad*. Whether or not you had a great biological father, chances are you don't talk enough to your heavenly Father. For whatever reason, you don't depend on Him nearly enough. But if you think about the ups and downs of life—your needs, your desire to make a difference in the world, your deep craving for connection and hope—you really want to. Simply put, I dare you to pray.

- *Deliberate*: Notice the basic elements of Daniel's prayer in Daniel 9. He started with worship, recognizing God's character and attributes (v. 4, and along the way in vv. 7, 9, and 14). Then he confessed his sins and the sins of God's people (vv. 5–16). Finally, he made his supplications—his strong prayers of request (vv. 17–19). This is a good template for your prayers too.
- *Defy Normal*: Use Daniel's prayer as a model for speaking to God: worship and praise, confession, supplication, and gratitude. Don't think of it as some mechanical,

prescribed prayer, but rather taking on an attitude that pleases God. When you talk to God like this, you're basically saying, "God, You're great and truly awesome! I've messed up some things; please forgive me and help me make them right. I need Your help with some hard things going on in my life and in the lives of my family, friends, Christian brothers and sisters, and my community and world. Thanks for caring about all of this and for loving me. Talk to You soon." In a nutshell: *Wow! Sorry. Help? Thanks.* Give it a shot.

- *Deliberate*: On one hand, it's never too late to pray—God is always there, listening and caring. But too often, we pray "tomato frog" prayers—too little, too late, after the damage has already been done.
- *Defy Normal*: Pray proactively. When you know something important is coming up—a big meeting or project, a doctor's appointment, a ministry or business opportunity, Christmas—start praying now, and keep praying. It's more than good habit—it's a pathway to the peace and power of God's presence in your life.

- *Deliberate*: Strong prayer is a four-stranded rope of adoration, confession, petition, and holy motivation. It aligns you with God's will and develops in you the proper motives for praying, but just as importantly, it brings you into His presence. Daniel didn't just survive the challenges he faced; he thrived in them, and his active, ongoing relationship with God in prayer was a key factor.

- *Defy Normal*: Be a bell ringer. Need something? Ask God. Do it as often as you think of it, even if your prayer is just a brief one. Few things in the world defy normal like regular prayer. Try talking to God like that for a day—hey, try it for a whole week!—and see what difference it makes. Beyond the everyday benefit of developing your relationship with your Father in heaven, you'll have a crucial structure in place to help seek God when a trial or crisis strikes.

- *Deliberate*: Praying on behalf of others—intercession—is the remedy for self-absorption. It's typical of God's economy that when you invest time in someone else, you don't lose time; you gain perspective. Intercession also moves you away from a "bless me" mentality, as well as gossip, slander, and complaining.

- *Defy Normal*: Do the hard work of intercession. How many people do you know who would have no one praying for them if not you? Keep a running list—use a stack of Christmas cards or the contacts in your phone—and talk to God on their behalf regularly.

CHAPTER SIX

GET ON YOUR KNEES
AND FIGHT

COURAGE

Did you come across any bullies in grade school? I did. I specifically remember a particular bully during my sixth grade year. He would push me and get up in my face. He wanted to fight, and despite my best attempts to avoid it, I knew a conflict was inevitable. So one day I was alone in the restroom, and in walked this guy. He started pushing me, and I could feel myself getting all red-faced. I doubled up my fist and got ready to rumble, as I was tired of his incessant bullying. That's when he said to me, "You wouldn't hit a guy with glasses, would you?"

I decked him. Right to the boys' bathroom floor.

Now, I don't condone that kind of behavior. As I recall, I may have even been suspended for that one-sided bathroom brawl. But as much as I wanted to steer clear of conflict, I just couldn't do it. I grew up with three older brothers who were definitely not pacifists. So there were certain altercations I could not avoid, no matter how hard I tried.

You may not know it, but you and I are a part of another type of unavoidable conflict. This one doesn't involve a bathroom bully, but rather someone much stronger, more tenacious, and far more sinister. This conflict doesn't allow for pacifists. There is no sitting this one out, and you can't simply walk away from it. This battle isn't a physical one involving fists and blood but is spiritual and unseen. It doesn't concern your body but targets your soul. And the reason you're in this conflict is simply because of the family you belong to. Because you're a child of the one true God, your enemy, the devil, is on the prowl (1 Peter 5:8). And you're a target in his crosshairs.

Interestingly, a Gallup poll noted that while most Americans say they believe in God, fewer admit to believing in a devil. Most believe in heaven, but fewer believe in hell, reflecting a belief of convenience, or what we *wish* to be true.[1] It seems like a lot of people are falling into the trap that C. S. Lewis described when he said, "There are two equal and opposite errors into which our race can fall about the devils. One is to disbelieve in their existence. The other is to believe, and to feel an excessive and unhealthy interest in them."[2]

So there's denial on one hand and obsession on the other. Some people flatly deny that there is any spiritual reality whatsoever. If they can't see it, it simply doesn't exist to them. But as any soldier will tell you, it's the enemy you *can't* see whom you have to worry about the most. If you have an enemy on the other side of the hill, and you don't know he's there, then he's got you exactly where he wants you and is therefore more dangerous. And then there are those who see the devil everywhere and in everything, even developing a sort of fascination with him. That's the kind of attention the devil loves.

> It's the enemy you *can't* see whom you have to worry about the most.

But there is a healthy balance between the extremes of denial and obsession when it comes to dealing with Satan. John White says about demons, "Have no delusions about their reality or their hostility. . . . They will also oppose you as you obey Christ. If you play it cool and decide not to be a fanatic about Christianity, you will have no trouble from them. But if you're serious about Christ being your Lord and God, you can expect opposition."[3]

PRAYING THROUGH CRISIS MANAGEMENT

Daniel was well acquainted with this cosmic bully called the devil. Daniel 10 begins with a problem. Something was bothering Daniel:

> In the third year of Cyrus king of Persia a message was revealed to Daniel, whose name was called Belteshazzar [his Babylonian name]. The message was true, but the

appointed time was long; and he understood the message, and had understanding of the vision. In those days I, Daniel, was mourning three full weeks. I ate no pleasant food, no meat or wine came into my mouth, nor did I anoint myself at all, till three whole weeks were fulfilled. (Daniel 10:1–3)

This experience took place toward the end of Daniel's life and career. He was around eighty-six or eighty-seven years of age. And it's no small thing when an eighty-six-year-old doesn't eat for three weeks. Daniel was not only an aged man; he also didn't have the physical strength he once had. Add to this the fact that he had been mourning, weeping, and fasting for those three weeks. But the question is: *Why* was he weeping? A clue is found in the phrase, "In the *third year* of Cyrus king of Persia."

Now here's why that's so important. The Jews had been back in Jerusalem for two years. This is something Daniel saw and prayed for in previous chapters. He had announced it and prayed for it, and now it had finally happened. We know from the book of Ezra that in the first year of Cyrus's reign, Cyrus gave an edict allowing the Jewish people to return to Jerusalem from Babylon. Now two years had passed following that return. What could have happened in those two years that caused Daniel to mourn and grieve?

Consider first of all that only a small portion of the Jewish people in Babylon actually returned to Jerusalem. Ezra 2:64-65 tells us almost fifty thousand Jews left Babylon and returned to Jerusalem. That number was a mere drop in the bucket compared to how many Jews chose to remain in Babylon. That alone was enough to send Daniel into mourning. God's people could have gone back home to the Promised Land, but they didn't want to. And why not? Why did they stay? They had gotten comfortable in Babylon. They had been there for a long time, raised kids there, and even become prosperous there. Worse, they had become absorbed into that pagan culture. So why uproot their families and rough it back to a place that was desolate? That didn't make sense to them. Of course, it didn't matter to them that God wanted them to come home. Sadly, they now considered Babylon to be their new home.

Not only that, but the Jews who did return hadn't been very successful. After being in Jerusalem for two years, they had yet to reestablish the Jewish monarchy. The returning Jews went back under the leadership of a guy named Zerubbabel (a man from the lineage of King David) to establish the monarchy once again. But when they got back, it took them seven months just to clear the rubble from the temple grounds. They were hassled and bullied by their enemies until the work came to a screeching halt.

So, here was Daniel, a man who had been praying and dreaming about his people returning to Jerusalem, but only a small percentage had chosen to do so. And those who had returned had failed to accomplish very much. So Daniel understandably went into a time of mourning, fasting, and praying.

By now we know prayer was a habit in Daniel's life. Whenever his heart was overwhelmed, he took it to the Lord . . . in prayer . . . on his knees. But this was no ordinary prayer time. Daniel was about to be let in on a cosmic battle, a fight in the heavens that spills over to the earth. And Daniel joined in that battle the moment he got on his knees. He engaged in prayer concerning his people's apathy, indifference, and worldliness. Daniel's bent knees were an outward picture of his submitted heart. We often think that to do battle we must stand up and fight. But Daniel knew something: his priority of getting down on his knees gave him a distinct advantage in spiritual warfare. That's so unlike the American church, isn't it? Whenever there's a spiritual battle, we call a committee meeting to discuss our options. Individual Christians do the same thing—only their "committee" is much smaller. They get their friends together to moan, groan, gripe, complain, or gossip—all the while they should be on their knees praying. Not Daniel. He had such a fight ahead of him that he knew he had to gear up for battle by getting on his knees.

The apostle Paul understood this. Writing about the role of prayer in spiritual warfare, he urged, "Pray in the Spirit at all times and on every occasion. Stay alert and be persistent in your prayers for all believers everywhere" (Ephesians 6:18 NLT).

William Cowper penned, "And Satan trembles, when he sees / the weakest saint upon his knees."[4] You can always do more than pray after you've prayed, but you really can't do more than pray *until* you've prayed.

Martin Luther, a man all too familiar with Satan's attacks, is rumored to have said on a very busy day, "I have so much to do that I shall spend the first three hours in prayer."[5]

COMMANDING PRESENCE OF A COMMANDING OFFICER

So Daniel was clued in on what was happening (or rather, *not* happening) back in Jerusalem, and it caused him to mourn, weep, fast, and pray. But suddenly heaven interrupted him. Daniel's problem was unexpectedly eclipsed by a *commanding presence*.

Now on the twenty-fourth day of the first month, as I was by the side of the great river, that is, the Tigris, I lifted my eyes and looked, and behold, a certain man clothed in linen, whose waist was girded with gold of Uphaz! His body was like beryl [a translucent or transparent gold color], his face like the appearance of lightning, his eyes like torches of fire, his arms and feet like burnished bronze in color, and the sound of his words like the voice of a multitude.

And I, Daniel, alone saw the vision, for the men who were with me did not see the vision; but a great terror fell upon them, so that they fled to hide themselves. Therefore I was left alone when I saw this great vision, and no strength remained in me; for my vigor was turned to frailty in me, and I retained no strength. Yet I heard the sound of his words; and while I heard the sound of his words I was in a deep sleep on my face, with my face to the ground. (Daniel 10:4–9)

Remember, at this time Daniel was roughly eighty-six years old. He had seen an eyeful in his lifetime—dreams, visions, miraculous deliverances, and so forth. He had even interpreted other people's dreams and visions. But his physical heart was not what it used to be. And now this supernatural luminescent being stood in front of him, and Daniel collapsed. The men who were with Daniel were scared to death and hightailed it out of Dodge. This perfectly illustrates, among other things, the problem humanity has when interacting with heavenly beings. When an earthly being encounters the supernatural, it's typically traumatic to the mind and spirit. Every now and then, somebody appears on Christian television and says, "I saw God, and I've written a book about it." And I think, *If you ever really saw God, either you'd be dead or severely traumatized by His glory and holiness. And you'd certainly be a whole lot more humble about it.*

We know this because those in Scripture who experienced such divine encounters had this kind of reaction. Job said to the Lord, "I have heard of You by the hearing of the ear, but now my eye sees You. Therefore I abhor myself, and repent in dust and ashes" (Job 42:5–6). *That's* what happens when you see God. When Isaiah saw God, he said, "Woe is me, for I am undone! Because I am a man of unclean lips" (Isaiah 6:5). And how did Peter react when he discovered who Jesus really was? He said, "Depart from me, for I am a sinful man, O Lord!" (Luke 5:8). In other words, "I can't even hang out with You." And in Revelation 6, we see unbelievers begging the mountains and the rocks to "fall on us and hide us from the face of Him who sits on the throne and from the wrath of the Lamb!" (v. 16).

Daniel's response was equally devastated. He collapsed when he was exposed to this heavenly being. So who was this "certain man" Daniel saw? Some have suggested it's one of the angels Gabriel or Michael, both of whom are mentioned in the book of Daniel. Others say it's an angel of equal rank but whose name we do not know. However, to me the context and cross-references point to only one person: the preincarnate Christ. You may be aware that in the Old Testament we see the phrase "the Angel of the LORD" fifty times. This "Angel" is often addressed as "the Lord" and is even worshipped as God.

In Revelation 1, John heard a voice that said,

"I am the Alpha and the Omega, the Beginning and the End," says the Lord, "who is and who was and who is to come, the Almighty." . . .

Then I turned to see the voice that spoke with me. And having turned I saw seven golden lampstands, and in the midst of the seven lampstands One like the Son of Man, clothed with a garment down to the feet and girded about the chest with a golden band. His head and hair were white like wool, as white as snow, and His eyes like a flame of fire; His feet were like fine brass, as if refined in a furnace, and His voice as the sound of many waters; He had in His right hand seven stars, out of His mouth went a sharp two-edged sword, and His countenance *was* like the sun shining in its strength. And when I saw Him, I fell at His feet as dead. But He laid His right hand on me, saying to me, "Do not be afraid; I am the First and the Last. I am He who lives, and was dead, and behold, I am alive forevermore. Amen." (vv. 8, 12–18)

This is obviously a clear description of Jesus Christ. It could be that John saw the *post-resurrected* Christ in His glory and Daniel saw the *preincarnate* Christ in His glory.

But why was Daniel given this particular vision of Jesus, and why *then*? In the chapters that follow, we see that Daniel was told about the future battles of Israel, both in the near future and in the far future, between Greece and Persia, Antiochus Epiphanes, Alexander the Great, and others. But he was also shown another kind of battle, a different kind of battle—a cosmic battle taking place in heavenly places. In fact it's this battle that largely determines all other battles and wars on earth. So, before giving Daniel prophecies concerning those epic future battles, God wanted Daniel to know exactly who is in charge, who is the commanding officer.

You may remember the battle of Jericho in the book of Joshua. Just prior to taking that city, Joshua turned to see the same man, the Angel of the LORD, standing with His sword exposed, lifted up. Joshua asked, "Are You for us or for our adversaries?" (Joshua 5:13). The man's answer was classic: "No, but as Commander of the army of the LORD I have now come" (v. 14). The Bible says Joshua fell down and worshipped. And this person, whom I believe to be the preincarnate Christ, said, "Take your sandal off your foot, for the place where you stand is holy" (v. 15). There was to be worship before warfare—and the warfare didn't just comprise earthly armies, but also included heavenly entities.

Joshua saw the commanding officer, the Lord, in charge of the battle of Jericho. And here Daniel needed to see who was in charge of the battle he was about to get the details of. In the daily spiritual battles you and I face, we had better know who our commanding officer is, or we're going to get bloodied and beaten. That's why Hebrews 12 encourages us to be "looking unto Jesus, the author and finisher of our faith" (v. 2).

Unfortunately, when we go through hard times, especially spiritual battles, our tendency is to *gaze* at our problems and merely *glance* at the Lord. We think, *This is tough. This is horrible.* And panic sets in. Then we quickly glance at the Lord and shoot up an emergency prayer: "Help me, Lord!" But there's a big difference between a gaze and a glance. Wouldn't it be great if we could switch those around and begin *glancing* at our problems and *gazing* at the Lord?

As you go through life, you will typically achieve whatever you focus on. You will hit what you're aiming at. In golf you should keep your head down and your eye on the ball, but often you look down the fairway too soon, only to discover that you failed to hit that little white ball correctly. Similarly, if you are focusing on your problems and just giving the Lord an occasional glance, you're essentially giving your problems permission to control you. They will pretty much define your life and set your level of contentment. But if you're gazing at the Lord and only glancing at your problems, you'll develop solid footing for spiritual warfare. Get a good view of your commanding officer and notice His strength, confidence, and ability. Now you're ready for battle.

That's what you really need. But is it what you really *want*?

We've seen the problem of Daniel's people, and the commanding presence of the preincarnate Christ. Finally, let's look at the powers contending against him.

THE WAR BEHIND THE BATTLE

The story continues:

> Suddenly, a hand touched me, which made me tremble on my knees and on the palms of my hands. And he said

to me, "O Daniel, man greatly beloved, understand the words that I speak to you, and stand upright, for I have now been sent to you." While he was speaking this word to me, I stood trembling.

Then he said to me, "Do not fear, Daniel, for from the first day that you set your heart to understand, and to humble yourself before your God, your words were heard; and I have come because of your words." (Daniel 10:10–12)

In other words, he was saying, "Three weeks ago when you started fasting and praying, your prayer was answered in heaven, and I was sent to you."

"But the prince of the kingdom of Persia withstood me twenty-one days; and behold, Michael, one of the chief princes, came to help me, for I had been left alone there with the kings of Persia. Now I have come to make you understand what will happen to your people in the latter days, for the vision refers to many days yet to come."

When he had spoken such words to me, I turned my face toward the ground and became speechless. And suddenly, one having the likeness of the sons of men touched my lips; then I opened my mouth and spoke, saying to him who stood before me, "My lord, because of the vision my sorrows have overwhelmed me, and I have retained no strength. For how can this servant of my lord talk with you, my lord? As for me, no strength remains in me now, nor is any breath left in me."

Then again, the one having the likeness of a man touched me and strengthened me. And he said, "O man greatly beloved, fear not! Peace be to you; be strong, yes, be strong!"

So when he spoke to me I was strengthened, and said, "Let my lord speak, for you have strengthened me."

Then he said, "Do you know why I have come to you? And now I must return to fight with the prince of Persia; and when I have gone forth, indeed the prince of Greece will come. But I will tell you what is noted in the Scripture of Truth. (No one upholds me against these, except Michael your prince.)" (10:13–21)

In the Bible there are specific designations of certain people. For example, Abraham is called "the friend of God" (James 2:23), David was called "a man after [God's] own heart" (Acts 13:22), and Jesus called John the Baptist the greatest man born of women (Matthew 11:11). But did you know there are only two people in the entire Bible given the title "greatly beloved"? One was Daniel, and the other was the apostle John, who is called the disciple "whom Jesus loved" (John 20:2). Interestingly, both Daniel and John were the ones who wrote apocalyptic books in the Bible. The book of Daniel even parallels much of Revelation's prophecies.

So do you get the picture here? As soon as Daniel began praying, help was sent from heaven but was roadblocked for three weeks by a character dubbed "the prince of the kingdom of Persia" (Daniel 10:13). That's why Daniel had been fasting and mourning for three weeks. And who was this prince of Persia? From a purely human perspective, it would appear to be Cyrus, king of Persia. However, the particular prince referenced in this vision is not a human being, because it required two supernatural angels to fight against him for a considerable amount of time. What we witness in this passage is the curtain being pulled back for Daniel to see into the real world of cosmic warfare, the world of demons and angels.

Though Persia did have a human *king* (Cyrus), there was also a demonic *prince* behind that king, empowering him. This shouldn't surprise us. Jesus said that Satan is "the ruler of this world" (John 12:31), and Paul called Satan "the prince of the power of the air, the spirit who now works in the sons of disobedience" (Ephesians 2:2). A few chapters later Paul talked about "principalities" and "powers" (Ephesians 6:12). So, demonic forces are very real and involved in the affairs of humankind.

This truth gives us great insight into the nature of the spiritual battle we are in. There is a God and there also is a devil. And this devil is accompanied by a host of demonic forces. The Bible tells us that Satan drew a third of the angels out of heaven when he rebelled against God (Revelation 12:4). How many is that? I'm not sure, but Revelation describes the angels around the throne of God, numbering them at "ten thousand times ten thousand, and thousands of thousands" (Revelation 5:11). So that's at least a hundred million, plus a bunch more. And a third of their original number fell from heaven, becoming a well-organized network whose chief desire is to thwart God's plan and hinder God's people (that's *you*!). Knowing this helps us better understand Paul's words in Ephesians 6: "We do not wrestle against flesh and blood, but against principalities, against powers, against the rulers of the darkness of this age, against spiritual hosts of wickedness in the heavenly places" (v. 12).

Daniel 10 seems to imply that certain demons are assigned to nations and/or geographical and political territories. In this case, one was assigned to Persia and another assigned to Greece. It makes you wonder what the prince of San Francisco must be like, or the prince of Las Vegas. Or the prince of Washington, DC, or of your city. First John 5:19 reminds us, "The whole world lies under the sway of the wicked one." Think about all that's going on in the world right now, all the evil, murder, terrorism, and ungodliness. All this is merely the spillover from the unseen world and a glimpse into the invisible battle that's taking place every day in the heavens.

The demons that fell with Satan (Revelation 12:3–4) constitute a force of spirit beings who went from being holy before

God to being evil, malevolent beings cast out of God's presence. That rebellion is given more detail in Isaiah 14 and Ezekiel 28. Ever since that time, demons have shown up in human society. As believers we understand a reality that most are completely oblivious to—that we human beings are not the only intelligent beings in the universe. We've got company! We inhabit the material world, but angels, both holy and fallen, inhabit the spiritual world. The history of the world—with all the nations' conflicts and struggles—is in the crossfire of the battle.

When the New Testament opened and Jesus came on the scene as the promised Jewish Messiah and Savior of the world, the demons stepped up their activity to a whole new level. That makes sense. They had always known that a Deliverer was coming to spell their doom, so when Jesus arrived, their organized movement was ratcheted up to a fever pitch. They have been active ever since, trying to convince unbelievers to stay in their unbelief or religious disguise and trying to keep believers from being too serious about following Christ. That's why Paul told us to "put on the whole armor of God, that you may be able to stand against the wiles of the devil . . . praying always with all prayer and supplication in the Spirit" (Ephesians 6:11, 18).

Daniel prayed and got a whole a lot more than he bargained for, including revelation of future battles and insight into a spiritual battle between angels and demons. It makes me wonder why we piddle around with such petty things in life when God wants us to know monumental truths. We spend so much time with trivial, day-to-day distractions when there's so much more to what's really going on around us. When Paul told the Ephesians to "stand" against the devil and his minions, he used a military word that indicates holding a vital defensive position while being under attack. He even explained the military-like organization in the demonic armies similar to colonels, lieutenants, sergeants, and privates when he divided them into *principalities, powers, rulers,* and *hosts of wickedness* (Ephesians 6:12). These are rankings within the demonic empire and the hierarchy by which demons carry out Satan's counterstrategies against God's plans. There is a certain level of sophistication and efficiency among these malevolent ranks. We find ourselves in the precarious place of being pitted against an incredibly powerful and well-organized enemy.

This is not an app. It's not a game on your iPad. This is life in its clearest reality. Believer, you are part of a very real spiritual conflict. You may not even be aware of it, which of course means the devil has you right where he wants you. But now you know! And instead of that discouraging you, you should be encouraged. Think of it. A third of the angels followed Satan, but two-thirds of the angels still serve God. So right at the start, Satan is already outnumbered. Further, the Bible says, "He who is in you [God] is greater than he who is in the world [Satan]" (1 John 4:4). So you're on the winning side, no matter what, or who, comes your way.

ESSENTIAL PREPARATION FOR SPIRITUAL BATTLE

But to survive and effectively engage in this spiritual fight, there are two very important things Daniel wanted us to know.

THE IMPORTANCE OF SCRIPTURE

The first thing we need to be prepared with in spiritual battle is *the importance of Scripture*. Notice what this angelic being said to Daniel: "But I will tell you what is noted in the Scripture of Truth" (Daniel 10:21). Elsewhere the Bible is called "the sword of the Spirit" (Ephesians 6:17) and even a weapon that's "sharper than any two-edged sword" (Hebrews 4:12). It is both a defensive weapon as well as an offensive one. It can deflect an attack as well as inflict an attack.

According to the Bible, the devil is the one "who *deceives* the whole world" (Revelation 12:9). Deception is one of the main arrows Satan fires from his bow. For a Christian, knowing Scripture is essential. It's like a surgeon knowing how to operate, a football player knowing the playbook, or a musician knowing how to play a song. It's nonnegotiable. You simply can't face life each day without feeding, nourishing, and equipping yourself with the Word of God. Cut the Bible out of your life, and you are *guaranteed* to become a casualty of war. Carry the Bible into your battles and you're sure to gain the upper hand.

The Word of God is so potent that it can transform people

from the realm of spiritual darkness to light, from falsehood to truth, from being deceived to being enlightened. Every time God's Word leads you out of temptation or through a trial, it's a demonstration of Scripture's power to cut through the spiritual and moral blindness inflicted by satanic forces. Every time that same Word of Truth leads a person to salvation, it demonstrates its power to cut a swath through Satan's dominion and bring life to a soul previously sentenced to death.

THE IMPORTANCE OF PRAYER

The second thing Daniel taught us is *the importance of prayer.* Like Daniel, when you're on your knees, you are on the front lines of battle. Prayer is like bringing a gun to a knife fight. No wonder the deceiver wants to keep you from engaging in prayer at all costs. When you're in prayer, the devil is defeated. We are on the winning side, and we get to use the big guns! What an awesome God! And if He is for us, who can be against us? (Romans 8:31).

As far as the ultimate war is concerned, we can't lose. Our commanding officer dealt the defeating blow while on the cross (Colossians 2:14–15). He bound the strong man because He is stronger (Luke 11:22–23). That means that nothing will be able to snatch you away from God's love, His care, and His plan (John 10:28). But you can lose skirmishes along the way. That's where prayer comes in—and that's where Daniel entered the battle.

Daniel understood that this demonic global conspiracy is bigger, stronger, and more organized than he could face on his own. So he didn't. Daniel tapped into the power of the stronger one; he revealed his dependence on the Lord, whose battle it is. It's interesting that after Paul listed the armor for spiritual warfare in Ephesians 6—the belt of truth, the breastplate of righteousness, the shoes of the gospel of peace, the shield of faith, the helmet of salvation, and the sword of the Spirit—he then mentioned prayer (v. 18). Why? Because even when we are well equipped for battle, we're still dependent on God.

WHAT TO PRAY FOR

What things do you pray for in a spiritual battle? Pray for *perseverance*—the ability to stay steady, keep going, and not quit. Pray for *wisdom* not to waste this opportunity to display God's grace as others are watching you face these difficulties. And pray for *others*, including fellow believers who are also fighting skirmishes on their own fronts. Finally, pray for *victory*. If you fight the battle the way God wants you to fight it, armed with His truth and depending on Him in prayer, He will give you a victory you have never known before. Your greatest joys will come from the greatest victories enjoyed after your greatest battles.

> Even when we are well equipped for battle, we're still dependent on God.

Our battle is real and our enemy is powerful, so we have to

always be ready to rumble. And nothing makes Satan weak in the knees more than when we are *on* our knees. So pray!

In 1857, slavery, rebellion, and rumors of war were spreading across the United States. Three years later, Americans turned on each other and made bloody history. But in that same year, another kind of history was being made in New York City. It's the kind of history you don't read about in textbooks.

On September 23, 1857, a Christian layman named Jeremiah Lanphier held his first ever businessman's prayer meeting in Lower Manhattan. It was not, by any account, a rousing success. He had passed out fliers for weeks—and only six men attended. Two weeks later the stock market crashed, and thousands of families lost all they had. Ironically, this time also marked the beginning of one of the greatest spiritual awakenings the world has ever seen. Week by week, Jeremiah Lanphier's tiny lunch-hour prayer meeting grew larger and larger. By December, his six men had grown to ten thousand, and they met not every week, but every *day*.

The New York newspapers took notice, and when word spread to other cities, spontaneous revival broke out across the country. In Cleveland and Saint Louis, thousands packed downtown churches and theaters three times each day just to pray. In Chicago, churches had waiting lists for people wanting to teach Sunday school. And all across America pastors were baptizing twenty thousand new believers every week.

This revival became known as the Third Great Awakening

and eventually spread around the world. In England entire towns were converted. Some towns disbanded their police force because of a lack of crime, and so many people came to Christ that churches were forced to hold services outside to accommodate the swelling crowds. The world had seen nothing like it—before or since. It was revival on a global scale. And God started it with *one man*.

So what do you think? Can history repeat itself? Could it happen again? Daniel was just one person. And so are you. But according to God, one person and prayer can move heaven and earth. Prayer is your supernatural power source. Your ammunition for victory.

Christian, get on your knees and fight . . .

. . . and *win*!

DARE TO DEFY N⁰RMAL: COURAGE

Fighting is never fun, but sometimes it's necessary. Certainly, that's the case with the Christian life: *It's not a playground but a battleground.* Spiritual warfare (the cosmic battle between forces of good and evil) is a reality that none can escape but few really understand. For Daniel, the curtain was pulled back and he was allowed to see past the natural world into the realm of the supernatural. It takes discernment to know when to fight, instruction to know how, and courage to do so. Many playground fights have begun with a dare, but I dare you to look past the veil of this world and see your true enemy—a foe that only God can defeat and a battle that you can fight only on your knees. I dare you to trust God and have the courage to fight.

- *Deliberate*: You wouldn't leave the house without getting dressed, but how often have you gone out without talking to God about the day ahead? Some day's battles are bigger than others, but they all matter. In fact, it's how you handle the small, everyday things that determines how you handle the big events.

- *Defy Normal*: Gear up for battle by getting on your knees. Switch around the typical perspective and *gaze* at God while only *glancing* at your problem. You learn to do that by making it a priority. When you get up tomorrow, talk to God. Acknowledge that He is your commanding officer. Ask Him to help you keep His strength and ability in mind as you face the day. Arm yourself by knowing His Word and trusting in His grace. Then go about your day with confidence in Him. It takes practice, but it prepares you for the day's challenges like nothing else.

- *Deliberate*: Spiritual warfare is real. Yes, God exists, but so does Satan. However, contrary to the world's view, they are not equal counterparts; God allows the devil and his minions to work in the world. But the Bible says that you can overcome these spirits that are "not of God . . . because He who is in you is greater than he who is in the world" (1 John 4:3–4). You fight from a position of ultimate victory.

- *Defy Normal*: Know your enemy. Read these passages about Satan and his fate: Matthew 25:41, Revelation 12:12, and Revelation 20:10. What do these verses tell you about Satan's anger and aggression? All the more reason to prepare for each day by focusing on God and asking Him to be your shield and your sword.

- *Deliberate*: The world is largely oblivious to the true nature of the ongoing battle in the spiritual realm. It started with Satan's fall (see Revelation 12:3–4, Isaiah 14, and Ezekiel 28 for more details), but it has continued throughout history and will continue until Jesus returns.

- *Defy Normal*: Know your weapons. Most of your spiritual weapons are defensive (Ephesians 6:13–18), others, offensive (Ephesians 6:17 and Hebrews 4:12). Your primary weapon in both cases is God's Word. You need to know it, both to be of use to God in the battle and to avoid becoming a casualty yourself. Your next move is to pray regularly. Ask God for perseverance, wisdom, the success of other believers, and victory. Remember, if God is for you, who can be against you (Romans 8:31)?

- *Deliberate*: When it comes to spiritual warfare, don't get lost in the details. Since the human tendency is either to deny the devil's existence or to obsess over him, stick to the simple truth: you cannot defeat Satan, but God through Jesus Christ already has. Unbelievers aren't even aware that a battle is going on because the "god of this age [Satan] has blinded the minds of unbelievers" (2 Corinthians 4:4 NIV), but you can ask other believers to step up with you in the fight, whether the problem is deeply personal or broadly global.

- *Defy Normal*: Know your tactics. When Satan comes knocking, send Jesus to answer the door. Anticipate the enemy's attacks, both generally and specifically.

  - Generally, ask God to prepare you for attacks you couldn't possibly anticipate. Military history tells us that many a battle was lost because officers didn't anticipate a surprise maneuver by enemy forces, and soldiers will tell you the enemy you can't see is the most dangerous.

  - Specifically, be brutally honest with yourself and list the ways that the devil could attack you, based on your weak spots—the things that tempt you, your temperament, your entertainment choices. Have the courage to shore up your defenses, knowing that being serious about Christ as your Lord makes you a target.

CHAPTER SEVEN

LOOK OUT AND LOOK UP

HOPE

I once had a history professor who loved to remind his students of that famous George Santayana quote, "Those who cannot remember the past are condemned to repeat it."[1] I remember him referencing that quote at least once a week; it almost seemed cliché after awhile. The more I think about it, the more that observation rings true to me. For example, have you noticed that every generation thinks *they're* the most unique generation that has ever lived? They try so hard to do things totally differently than their parents did, yet when they grow up and have kids, they typically repeat the same things their parents did. Patterns of behavior, trends, and styles do tend to repeat themselves, reminding me of another oft-quoted saying: "What goes around comes around."

If anything, my history professor only hinted at the

problem: human beings seem to be incapable of learning anything from the past, at least when it comes to changing the way we behave. Historians have all kinds of theories about the kinds of cycles of civilizations hinted at in the vision that God gave Nebuchadnezzar (Daniel 2:26–45). One scholar made a study of eleven different nations down through history and found a pattern repeated in each of them to different degrees over a three-thousand-year period. He summarized them like this:

> The stages of the rise and fall of great nations seem to be: The Age of Pioneers (outburst), the Age of Conquests, the Age of Commerce, the Age of Affluence, the Age of Intellect, the Age of Decadence. Decadence is marked by: defensiveness, pessimism, materialism, frivolity, an influx of foreigners, the Welfare State, a weakening of religion. Decadence is due to: Too long a period of wealth and power, selfishness, love of money [and] the loss of a sense of duty.[2]

Bingo.

And even if that seems too simplistic, it touches on a few important reminders: there's nothing new under the sun, and we tend to forget what has happened before our time.

No wonder God told His people in the Old Testament, "And you shall remember that the LORD your God led you all the way these forty years" (Deuteronomy 8:2).

But they didn't. And so, failing to learn from their past history, they unfortunately repeated it over and over again.

WHAT, ME WORRY?

So far we have seen that Daniel mourned, prayed, and fasted for three weeks. And when the answer to his prayers finally came, it wasn't what he expected. The Lord predicted even more pain, suffering, and sorrow for Israel all the way to the very end of history when Messiah's kingdom comes.

Now you may be wondering, *Why would God allow all this to happen? Aren't the Jews God's chosen people? Don't they have a special covenant relationship with God?* I'm pretty sure Daniel was thinking the same thing. But Daniel 11:35 gives us the answer: "And some of those of understanding shall fall, to refine them, purify them, and make them white, until the time of the end; because it is still for the appointed time."

In other words, God was going to use this suffering to purify Israel for Himself. Would you agree that few things are more effective in driving people to God than suffering? I know of nothing that gets our attention and drives our eyes upward like going through hard times. I hate hard times, and you probably do as well. If we could, we'd eradicate suffering in all of its forms today, right? But God actually uses suffering while at the same time superintending it. That's why Peter wrote that trials have come so that "the genuineness of your faith, being much more precious than gold that perishes, though it is tested by fire, may be found to praise, honor, and glory at the revelation of Jesus Christ" (1 Peter 1:7).

But why did God tell Daniel this? Why did this old man get this new revelation? I believe one of the reasons God sent this prophecy to Daniel was to reassure the survival of the Jewish people. Put plainly, the Jews shouldn't still exist. More than any other race or people groups, Jews have been hated, hassled, and hounded throughout history. Yet here they are. They remain with us. The survival of the Jewish people is nothing short of miraculous. Their existence is proof of God's covenant with them. Between the time of Daniel and Jesus, hundreds of thousands of Jews were taken captive as prisoners, sold as slaves, and killed by ungodly rulers and nations.

In 70 AD the Romans entered Jerusalem and, according to Jewish historian Josephus, killed 1.1 million Jews.[3] The emperor Constantine instituted harsh laws against Jews, including the death penalty if they tried to punish a Jewish person who converted to Christianity.[4] At the Council of Clermont in the sixth century, Jews were forbidden to hold public office.[5] In 633 AD with the rise of Islam in the Arabian Peninsula, Jews were slaughtered. This Islamic hatred of Jews is still going on today. During the crusades of the eleventh century, the motto was "Kill a Jew and save your soul." Sadly, many Jews were slaughtered in the name of Christ. In fourteenth-century Europe, Jews were blamed for the Black Death, and thousands of them were killed because of it.[6] In 1492, tens of thousands of Jews were forced to leave Spain or risk being burnt at the stake for being Jewish.[7]

More recently, during World War II, Adolf Hitler's Nazi regime exterminated six million Jews in the Holocaust.

There is no reason Jews should exist. But they do. Winston Churchill noted, "Some people like the Jews, and some do not. But no thoughtful man can deny the fact that they are, beyond any question, the most formidable and the most remarkable race which has appeared in the world."[8] Their existence today, indeed their thriving, is a reality because God has a special role for them in the future. With the absence of a homeland for two millennia, the Jewish people managed to stay together and even thrive in hostile lands and antagonistic societies.

So often in the Old Testament God said to the false gods, "I can do what you can't do. I'm going to predict the future." So every time God makes good on a promise He has made or fulfills a prophecy He has given, it should cause us to well up with faith. Henry Ward Beecher once said, "Every tomorrow has two handles. We can take hold of it with the handle of anxiety or the handle of faith."[9] Of course, most of us like to grab the handle of anxiety when it comes to thinking about the future. Let's be honest and admit that none of us knows what is going to happen in the future. But so what? God has the future and *your* future in His plan and in His hands. He is in charge and in control. Nothing takes God by surprise. He never panics or worries. And because you are under His protection, neither should you. Corrie ten Boom said it well: "Never be afraid to trust an unknown future to a known God."[10]

THE DIVINE CONTRADICTION

The world is full of oxymorons (not just *morons*). I'm sure you know that an oxymoron is a phrase consisting of words that seem to contradict each other, like: *airline food, government organization, jumbo shrimp*, or *freezer burn*.

Allow me to challenge you with another oxymoronic phrase, this one a little closer to home. Here it is: *Dare to rest*.

It sounds strange, doesn't it? I mean, a dare implies doing something daring—that there is some element of danger or risk involved. But why would you have to dare someone to *rest*? Here's why. Somebody who is stressed out, a worrier, or an over-committed, workaholic, pedal-to-the-metal manager type is a person in desperate need of a break. Hence the challenge to slow down, pull over, and rest. Likewise, someone who is hearing bad news about the future, going through a painful time, also needs the exhortation to rest.

Why would you *rest*, though? Why wouldn't you do something about all the problems in your life, in the world? To a certain extent, it's good to care about your community and what's going on around the world. But I'm not saying to do nothing. I'm saying, *dare to rest*. Dare to trust that God will keep the world spinning while you take a breather. Because, really, when you rest, you're showing that you have hope. Resting in God's plan demonstrates hope in God's purpose. You're saying to yourself, to the rest of the world, and even to God, *I trust that God is in control, that He is good, that He will do what is right.*

Daniel the prophet was a man under stress. Having been given divine information about the future and bad news about his people, he had good reason to be consumed with worry from a human standpoint. Worry is commonplace—it's normal; it's the status quo. To defy that normal tendency, to rise above that level to a place of rest, is the Christian calling. Jesus said that when He is in control of your life, you "will find rest for your [soul]" (Matthew 11:29).

Study after study has revealed the correlation between resting in hope and managing stress. Spirituality is the best medicine for anxiety. Truly! It has been noted that "people who are more religious or spiritual use their spirituality to cope with life."[11] These are folks who quit trying to control things by themselves. They know there's Someone greater who is enacting a grander plan and purpose. The hope generated by such faith reduces stress and produces an inward calm. It can even decrease the average recovery time of hospitalized patients![12]

> Resting in God's plan demonstrates hope in God's purpose.

We live in a day and age when people are more stressed out than ever before. The average person is filled with anxiety, agitated by economic, social, and moral developments in this world. Some of us struggle just to get by week by week. Then you hear of what's going on in the Middle East and see turmoil, violence, and uncertainty filling our own country. Honestly, it makes you long for relief, for someone to come along and fix it all and make everything right, doesn't it? The very thought that such a thing is possible gives you hope.

And do we ever need it. Not only has there been a recent resurgence of anti-Semitism in Europe, but there is also a growing hostility toward Christians here in America. While believers are vilified in the media and increasingly marginalized in the marketplace, other Christians are being persecuted and martyred elsewhere in the world. But this is nothing compared to what is coming. I believe history is heading for a climactic intersection with prophecy. The book of Revelation describes a seven-year period known as the Great Tribulation when God will unleash His wrath on this rebellious planet. It will be an unprecedented time that will turn life as we know it into a hell on earth. During this period, one who is called by many names, but typically known as the "Antichrist," will rise (1 John 2:18), becoming a world leader. And his regime will force every human alive to worship him. Filled with a seething hatred for Christ, the Antichrist will spill the blood of all those who choose to trust in Jesus for salvation.

The Scriptures speak of the Tribulation as the very worst time the world will ever face. Daniel foresaw this as a "time of trouble, such as never was since there was a nation, even to that time" (Daniel 12:1). Jeremiah said that time of trouble will be so unique that "none is like it" (Jeremiah 30:7). Jesus affirmed this, adding, "For then there will be great tribulation, such as has not been since the beginning of the world until this time, no, nor ever shall be" (Matthew 24:21). He further stated that if He did not intervene, "no flesh would be saved" (Matthew 24:22).

These are significant statements considering all the atrocities and genocides throughout history. Think of it. The Great Chinese Famine from 1958 to 1962 killed thirty-six million people from combined natural disasters and the communist policies of Mao Zedong.[13] The reign of terror in Cambodia by the Khmer Rouge led by dictator Pol Pot in the 1970s took the lives of up to two million people.[14] World War II erupted from a hatred that resulted in the deaths of up to sixty million people.[15] The bubonic plague—called the Black Death—spread through Europe in the fourteenth century and killed about 60 percent of the population.[16] Approximately twenty million people died in five years![17] Other bleak periods could be mentioned, such as World War I and the Crusades. The coming Tribulation period will be worse than all of these. Hard to wrap your mind around that, isn't it?

However, I also believe the Scriptures teach us to hope, that they clearly teach that Jesus will return to rescue His bride, the church, those called out of the world system to salvation, prior to this time of judgment. God will rescue His people, just as He did with Noah and his family prior to the Flood judgment.

God has good aim, and He knows how to target His judgments. That's not to say we won't experience problems or consequences. Jesus plainly promised that "in the world you will have tribulation [trials and sorrows]" (John 16:33). But what's coming for the world is much different from day-to-day hardships and struggles. It will be tribulation from the hand of God Himself directed at the earth. The source of our daily hardship is the world system. The source of the coming Tribulation is God. Big difference!

Those Christians who are alive at that time will be spared the judgments God will reign down on the earth. Then, at the end of this seven-year Tribulation, something else will happen. That something is what Christians have been anticipating for the last two thousand years. Ever since Jesus taught His disciples to pray, "Thy kingdom come," we've been looking for His Second Coming. It's what Isaac Watts had in mind when he penned his famous hymn, "Joy to the world, the Lord is come! Let earth receive her king."

Revelation 19:11–16 paints the picture for us:

I saw heaven opened, and behold, a white horse. And He who sat on him was called Faithful and True, and in righteousness He judges and makes war. His eyes were like a flame of fire, and on His head were many crowns. He had a name written that no one knew except Himself. He was clothed with a robe dipped in blood, and His name is called The Word of God. And the armies in heaven, clothed in fine linen, white and clean, followed Him on white horses. Now out of His mouth goes a sharp sword, that with it He should strike the nations. And He Himself will rule them with a rod of iron. He Himself treads the winepress of the fierceness and wrath of Almighty God. And He has on His robe and on His thigh a name written:

KING OF KINGS AND
LORD OF LORDS.

And what of the beast, the Antichrist, the one who will terrorize the saints? Revelation 19 continues,

And I saw the beast, the kings of the earth, and their armies, gathered together to make war against Him who sat on the horse and against His army. Then the beast was captured, and with him the false prophet who worked signs in his presence, by which he deceived those who received the mark of the beast and those who worshiped his image. These two were cast alive into the lake of fire burning with brimstone. (vv. 19–20)

That's how the Antichrist comes to his end. And no one can help him because the one who will fight against him is God Himself.

"But wait," you may be asking. "What does all this have to do with Daniel?" Simple. There are significant portions of the book of Daniel that are prophecies dealing with the Antichrist, the Tribulation, and the Second Coming of Christ (as well as His first coming). Essentially the entire second half of the book of Daniel is devoted to these apocalyptic visions. So for Daniel, knowing both about his people's upcoming suffering as well as what takes place at the end of days could have potentially placed a huge burden of anxiety on him. It would be hard to hear and hard to live with that knowledge. But Daniel was comforted by what radio host Paul Harvey used to call "The Rest of the Story." And the rest of God's story is that He wins in the end—and His people are the winning team. It was this crowning truth that brought Daniel to unload these burdens consistently to God in prayer, releasing his worry to Him (Daniel 2:17–19; 6:10–11; 9:4–21). Only one word can fully describe such a response in the face of such uncertainty: hope. Daniel had hope because God promised that, in spite of all the hardship to come, things were going to work out.

And it's the same for us today. Remember what Jesus said in the Upper Room at the Last Supper, when the confused disciples were distressed about His prediction of impending death? Jesus wanted them to see beyond the immediate prediction and be comforted by the ultimate prediction—His return in glory and the heavenly home awaiting them.

He said, "Let not your heart be troubled; you believe in

God, believe also in Me. In My Father's house are many mansions; if it were not so, I would have told you. I go to prepare a place for you. And if I go and prepare a place for you, I will come again and receive you to Myself; that where I am, there you may be also" (John 14:1–3).

OUR BLESSED HOPE

Ever since Jesus uttered those words two thousand years ago, Christians of every age have been waiting for Him to come again, receive us to Himself, and return to take over the earth. This is the "blessed hope" that we've been longing for (Titus 2:13). So many hymns, so many songs have been written about the Second Coming. This is the ultimate reason to rest— Jesus is coming. And His return will

> Only one word can fully describe such a response in the face of such uncertainty: hope.

end all of the conflict against Israel, all of the pain and sorrow of the world, all of the oppression we've seen in Daniel's day and in ours.

Solomon wisely penned in Proverbs 21:1, "The king's heart is in the hand of the LORD, like the rivers of water; He turns it wherever He wishes." That was true with King Nebuchadnezzar, King Belshazzar, King Darius, and King Cyrus. It's been true with every world leader since that time.

If God can control a king, He can take care of you. Look at what Jesus told His disciples and closest friends:

Look at the birds of the air, for they neither sow nor reap nor gather into barns; yet your heavenly Father feeds them. Are you not of more value than they? Which of you by worrying can add one cubit to his stature?

So why do you worry about clothing? Consider the lilies of the field, how they grow: they neither toil nor spin; and yet I say to you that even Solomon in all his glory was not arrayed like one of these. Now if God so clothes the grass of the field, which today is, and tomorrow is thrown into the oven, will He not much more clothe you, O you of little faith?

Therefore do not worry, saying, "What shall we eat?" or "What shall we drink?" or "What shall we wear?" For after all these things the Gentiles seek. For your heavenly Father knows that you need all these things. But seek first the kingdom of God and His righteousness, and all these things shall be added to you. Therefore do not worry about tomorrow, for tomorrow will worry about its own things. Sufficient for the day is its own trouble. (Matthew 6:26–34)

Have you ever seen a worried bird? Ever catch a glimpse of a bird with its head in his claws fretting because he's anxious about the future? The image is laughable, right? Worry is a lot like a rocking chair: it gives you something to do but it won't get you anywhere. If God takes the time to care for the littlest birds of the air, feeding them and providing for generation after generation of the many varieties of avian species, will He not also care for you who are worth far more than they?

Have you ever thought about God in that way? Do you ever think about how much He loves you? How much He really cares about you? It takes relatively little effort to list all the bad things that happen to us in life. Those things could roll off the tongue at the drop of a hat. But have you ever stopped to consider what stress and suffering God may have kept from you? All the negative things that could have happened to you but didn't because His hand of protection was on you? Or have you spent much time learning to be like Daniel, who regularly practiced the art of unloading his burdens? It's the principle of *replacement.* Paul told the Philippians, "Be anxious for nothing, but in everything by prayer and supplication, with thanksgiving, let your requests be made known to God; and the peace of God, which surpasses all understanding, will guard your hearts and minds through Christ Jesus" (Philippians 4:6–7).

Did you get that? The way to experience rest (referred to as "peace" in this passage) is by replacing anxious responses with active requests. Replace your thoughts with God's truth. You may have to talk to yourself to get this done right. The psalmist did: "Why are you cast down, O my soul? And why are you disquieted within me? Hope in God" (Psalm 42:5).

This is good advice. In fact, it's a doctor's advice. D. Martyn Lloyd-Jones, a medical doctor turned pastor, offered this encouragement: "We must talk to ourselves instead of allowing 'ourselves' to talk to us. . . . Have you realized that most of your unhappiness in life is due to the fact that you are listening to yourself instead of talking to yourself?"[18] The New Testament calls this *taking your thoughts captive* (2 Corinthians 10:5 NASB). But it's more than just talking to yourself. It's telling the truth to yourself—*God's* truth—and then talking those truths over with God in prayer and supplication (a strong appeal, a wrestling with God over the issues you face). Remember, your uplook will determine your outlook. Make sure that you look far enough forward and upward to consider your ultimate and eternal reality.

CHOOSE TO REST

Worry and anxiety are easy to experience, but they eventually take a heavy toll on the body, mind, and soul. Like mileage on tires, they gradually erode your emotions, wearing them paper-thin. And like that balding tire, they soon burst, causing a breakdown. And who wants that in life?

Instead, why not choose, by faith . . . like Daniel . . . to *rest*? Do you have it rougher and tougher than he did? Are you in captivity? Have you been plucked out from your home to live in an openly pagan nation? Is your hometown in ruins? Have you been thrown into a pit of ravenous lions just because you love God? Not to downplay what we go through, but Daniel modeled this kind of faith in *the most difficult of times*.

And so can you.

You really can. Placing your full weight on the Father, roll your burden onto His strong shoulders. Can you think of any reason that you wouldn't want to pause, put down this book, and do that right now? Go ahead, I'll wait.

And why would you want to do that? Well, logically it makes perfect sense because Jesus can handle the weight much better than you can. But second, and most importantly, Peter confidently said you should do it because "He cares for you" (1 Peter 5:7). God is not just a supernatural burden-bearer. He's not merely some heavenly company you call to move some big spiritual boulder that's gotten lodged in your heart. He is powerful, but He is much more than that. No, the greatest reason to cast your burdens on Him is because He loves you very much and it delights Him to help you out.

Like any parent, nothing gives God more joy than to help you and be a Father to you. And our cries to Him are always met with mercy. Look at what the writer of Hebrews said: "For we do not have a High Priest who cannot sympathize with our weaknesses, but was in all points tempted as we are, yet without sin. Let us therefore come boldly to the throne of grace, that we may obtain mercy and find grace to help in time of need" (Hebrews 4:15–16).

Several words jump off the page to me in those verses—specifically *sympathize, grace, mercy,* and *help.*

Sympathize means God understands what we're going

through. Whatever you are facing, I challenge you to search the Gospels—especially the life, ministry, and death of Christ. There you will find Him facing similar circumstances and emotions. Know that He can honestly identify with you.

Grace is getting what we do not deserve. God's throne is called a "throne of grace," meaning He consistently lavishes us with His undeserved love and favor because of what Christ did for us.

Mercy has been defined as not getting what we *do* deserve. Because of sin, we deserve death, but God gives us life instead through Jesus. In fact, Paul wrote that there is not one drop of condemnation left for us (Romans 8:1). We are free and forgiven!

Help is the tangible aid that God pours out on us whenever we come to Him. As the psalmist reminded us, "God is our refuge and strength, a very *present help* in trouble. Therefore we will not fear, even though the earth be removed, and though the mountains be carried into the midst of the sea" (Psalm 46:1–2).

In other words, we don't just get the promise of heaven and a time when everything will get better. God's help is always *now* . . . in "the time of need" (Hebrews 4:16). When you're hurting, you need help immediately, and God has promised to be there for us and to never, ever forsake us (Hebrews 13:5). Jesus said He would be with us, "even to the end of the age" (Matthew

28:20). That may not mean our problems suddenly vanish or that our bank account is magically replenished, but it does mean we have His presence and power to deal with whatever comes our way, even if the earth itself is moved and mountains crumble into the sea! What tremendous hope we have in Jesus.

I love the story about the man who was in his boat out on the ocean when a storm came up. He wasn't too happy about that storm, because his boat was rocking back and forth and he didn't know if he was going to make it. But he remembered Psalm 121, which says, "He who keeps Israel shall neither slumber nor sleep" (v. 4). Thinking on that promise, "God never slumbers or sleeps," the man folded his hands, looked up to heaven, and said, "Well, God, since You don't ever rest, there's no sense in both of us losing sleep, so good night!"

What a way to look at life! You see, that's the kind of God we have. A God who stays awake in the storm so we don't have to worry about being capsized or drowning. He is a God who makes promises and faithfully keeps them while at the same time keeps us safely in His arms.

We can choose to look around us and be filled with fear and anxiety, or we can look up to God and be filled with faith and peace. It's our choice.

So I challenge you today: will you defy the status quo, embrace hope, and *dare to rest?*

DARE TO DEFY NORMAL: HOPE

There is nothing needed more in the world today than hope. Every generation faces the tendency toward despair and hopelessness. Daniel especially did since he was learning of his own people's future suffering that would last for generations. But at last, God gave him a precious ray of hope: the worst of times will usher in the best of times. Because Daniel had hope, he could rest in the face of great uncertainty, trusting God to keep His promises and carry out His plans for His people. So when I dare you to rest on God's promises, what I'm really daring you to do is hope.

- *Deliberate*: Few things drive people toward God like suffering. No one likes hard times, and with good reason—they're really hard. Ask most people what they'd change about the world, and they would most likely say, "End suffering. World peace. No more disease or hunger." All of that sounds pretty good, but without God, it's just wishful thinking. With God, though, even suffering takes on purpose, and that gives a hope that the world can't offer.

- *Defy Normal*: Practice the principle of replacement (Philippians 4:6–7). Replace your anxious responses to stress and suffering with active requests, and your thoughts with God's truth. Once you accept that God really loves you—the sparrows and lilies thing that Jesus was driving at (Matthew 6:26, 28–29)—trusting Him with your anxieties becomes a lot easier to practice.

- *Deliberate*: For unbelievers, the future has seldom seemed more uncertain. Environmental decline, terrorism, racism, addiction, and cultural shifts away from any kind of moral standard leave so many feeling hopeless. Daniel's vision, however, offers knowledge and hope. Jesus is coming back, and He will clean up this whole mess.

- *Defy Normal*: In uncertain times, hold fast to hope. As a believer in Christ, you are called to turn to Jesus and find rest for your soul (Matthew 11:29). When you feel the stress of the world setting in, take a moment to remind yourself of what the Bible says about the future. Yes, things will get more chaotic, but Jesus is coming back, first for His church and then to rule on earth. Give God thanks for His plans and provision in the future, and imagine the joy you will experience when you see Jesus face to face. Repeat as necessary, adding the biblical prayer, "Come soon, Lord Jesus" (1 Corinthians 16:22; Revelation 22:20).

- *Deliberate*: God has said that times will worsen— something that's easy to believe these days—but He has also said that He will preserve His people, that all people will live forever, and that He will reward those who faithfully serve Him.

- *Defy Normal:* It's hard to watch the news—it's depressing to see all the bad things going on in the world. There's a time to be aware of all that and to pray for people in their suffering, but as a believer, you have something more to offer: the hope of God in Christ. If everyone is going to live forever, it matters where. Be ready to share the hope of eternal life that Jesus offers. Pray that God will give you a chance to weigh in with that hope the next time the conversation shifts to the declining state of the world.

CHAPTER EIGHT

REACH UP,
IN, AND OUT

BALANCE

I once heard a story that illustrates an important point about balance—in both the literal and figurative senses. Apparently twenty-five-year-old Inge Brunner from Tuebingen, Germany, was visiting a friend in the hospital. Upon her arrival, Inge had the audacity to ask a doctor, "Is it okay if I smoke in here?"

"Absolutely not!" the doctor replied. "This is a hospital; and besides, it's highly unhealthy for you to smoke. You are forbidden to smoke in here!"

As the story goes, when the doctor left the room, Inge lit up a cigarette, opened the patient's window, and leaned out so as not to get any smoke inside. Unfortunately, she leaned a little too far and lost her balance, falling sixty-five feet to the ground below. However, her fall was broken by a tree—an *ash* tree (can you believe that?)—and she suffered only minor injuries. After walking back into the hospital, she announced, "I have learned my lesson. No more cigarettes for me." Her drastic lifestyle change occurred all because she simply lost her balance.[1]

Inge's experience teaches us an important life lesson: lose your balance, and you fall.

It's that simple.

Anytime you hear the word *balance*, it's common to feel a twinge of guilt, isn't it? I mean, we are trying so hard to balance so much in our busy lives. Things like our time, work, family, exercise, sleep, marriage, career, relationships, kids, sports, hobbies, church activities . . . and the list seems to go on and on. And on top of all that, we also have to balance our finances.

Lose your balance, and you fall.

It can wear you out just thinking about all the things you need to manage and balance. Most people feel a little guilty that their lives aren't quite balanced *enough*. Something or some part of our lives always seems a bit out of whack, overemphasized, or off-balance. In fact, it's rare to find a man or a woman who believes his or her life is in perfect balance. In my life, I've had seasons of imbalance when I've worked too much and rested too little, and seasons when I rested too much and worked too little. That's why it's so motivating to look at the life of Daniel, a man who actually achieved what could honestly be called a balanced life.

If you're going to model yourself after someone, whether it's for fitness, finances, or family, doesn't it make sense to follow someone who's actually been successful? Would you take financial investment advice from a person who's never made any money? Or fitness instruction from someone who's grossly out of shape? Of course not. You want to follow a proven winner.

Daniel was a winner. A champion. And as we survey his life, we see four areas where he achieved balance and success.

ARMS UP AND HANDS OUT

First, Daniel worshipped God supremely, yet he was also involved socially. That's quite a balancing act. We see this delicate balancing act back in Daniel 1:8. It's really the key that opens the entire book: "Daniel purposed in his heart that he would not defile himself with the portion of the king's delicacies, nor with the wine which he drank."

In this verse, we discover the secret to Daniel's life and effectiveness. Here was this teenager, displaced in Babylon, who made a core value statement that defined his life direction. "Purposed in his heart" simply means Daniel made a choice. He made a decision right then and there that formed the basis for his influence in the rest of the book. In fact, his effectiveness or ineffectiveness in life depended on this choice. W. A. Criswell once said, "All of life is filled with crises and decisions. Almost every day there will be a fork in the road. Where you are today is because of the turn in the road that you took yesterday."[2]

So young Daniel made his choice—to love God supremely. "I'm all in for God. He's number one in my life, and I'm not going to let anything mess with that."

Now that's a purpose-driven life! As a young man Daniel was determined to defy normal and rise above the status quo. He chose to keep step with heaven rather than earth, to be distinct, to not go along with the crowd and be corrupted by ungodly influences. Not only that, but he stuck with that commitment throughout his life, so that by the time we get to chapter 6, when Daniel was in his eighties, we see that he was persecuted because of that purposeful worship of God. Remember what he did when he was told not to worship God? He opened his windows so everybody could see him. And three times a day, facing Jerusalem, Daniel got on his knees and prayed to the very God he had unswervingly committed to years earlier.

Daniel was an amazing man who refused to be intimidated by powerful people or be afraid of difficult circumstances. The Babylonians could change his address, his name, and his education, but they could not change his heart or his belief system. His theology was intact and safe from contamination by false beliefs or ungodly behavior. Why? Because he "purposed in his heart." But here's where the balance kicks in.

At the same time Daniel was worshipping God supremely, he was also involved socially. This intensely spiritual man was effectively engaged in his culture. His commitment to God spilled over and made an impact on the people around him.

Remember, chapter 1 tells us that "in all matters of wisdom and understanding" Daniel and his buddies were "ten times better" than any of the rest who were in the court (1:20). And his wisdom and understanding were the reason he was promoted in the very next chapter. "The king promoted Daniel . . . and he made him ruler over the whole province of Babylon" (2:48). Daniel's sense of balance led to being chosen for a key political position in his culture. And this became the pattern of his life, making him impressive to later rulers and useful for the subsequent kingdoms of Belshazzar, Darius, and Cyrus: "Daniel prospered in the reign of Darius and in the reign of Cyrus the Persian" (6:28).

Daniel was not a religious recluse but a man who was involved in his culture. That's inspiring to me. I believe this generation could use a few more dedicated believers in places of social and political responsibility, don't you? This world needs men and women who influence culture while maintaining spiritual integrity. Daniel did that. He struck a balance between worship and work, or what some refer to as *upreach* and *outreach*. Jesus Christ did the same thing. He came to this earth principally to bring salvation, or in His own words, "to seek and to save that which was lost" (Luke 19:10). Nobody will dispute that. He didn't come to just be a nice guy and set a good example. He came to save people from their sin. However, at the same time, one of His own apostles noted, "God anointed Jesus of Nazareth with the Holy Spirit and with power, who went about doing good and healing all who were oppressed by the devil" (Acts 10:38). Jesus was saving souls, but He was also helping people around Him, and by doing do, He attracted them to eternal salvation.

Other notable people throughout church history have done the same as Daniel. John Wesley was one of them. Now, if you know church history, you've heard of John Wesley. Wesley was an itinerant evangelist who is credited with founding the Methodist Church. But what you may not know about John Wesley is that he also took up certain social causes during his time, the most noble of them being the abolition of slavery, human trafficking, and the elimination of the African slave trade. The mistreatment of animals was another, along with public drunkenness. He interfaced with a political man named William Wilberforce, also a committed believer. Several days before Wesley died in 1791, he wrote a letter to William Wilberforce, then a member of Parliament. In the letter, he urged Wilberforce to end the slave trade, saying, "Unless God has raised you up for this very thing, you will be worn out by the opposition of men and devils. But if God be for you, who can be against you?"[3] Wesley encouraged him not to become weary in well doing. That's the essence of worshipping God supremely while also being involved socially.

We evangelicals have a tendency to be escapists, using the church to hide from the world. Sure, we go on occasional raids into enemy territory, and where the drawbridge goes down, we cross over the moat and have our Christian event. But then we quickly run back into the safety of the castle. However, as believers, we have a human responsibility to fulfill Jesus' divine commission. We are not to be "of the world" (John 17:14), but we are definitely to be in it. Daniel was that kind of guy.

He was both salt and light. He was salt, used by God as a preservative to deter the cultural decay of his time. I believe we can also be used in our culture to impede the corruption that naturally occurs in a sin-filled world. But Daniel wasn't just salt; he was also light. He shone the luminous glory of God's power and providence in Babylon and in the courts of kings, leading people out of spiritual darkness, allowing them see the true God.

Daniel struck a balance—he worshipped God supremely but stayed involved socially.

STANDING AND WALKING

Another area of balance in Daniel's life was that he stood alone, yet he walked with others. I am continually impressed as I read the book of Daniel, because he was never afraid to stand alone if he felt like God wanted him to. Daniel was willing to act alone, remaining true to his convictions. For example, in chapter 1, Daniel acted alone in pro-testing the king's diet, which was being imposed on everybody. He said, "I don't want to do that," then "*We* don't want to do

> Daniel struck a balance—he worshipped God supremely but stayed involved socially.

that," as he became the spokesman for the other Jewish youths. So they embarked on their special fast.

In chapter 2, it was Daniel alone who approached Arioch the captain of the guard, and eventually the king, saying, "I'll give you my guarantee; I will interpret that dream for you." In chapter 5, Daniel alone stood against Belshazzar. In chapter 6, he stood alone against the prayer ban, and he alone faced the lions' den. Over and over again, Daniel made an uncompromising stand, sometimes doing it all alone. But here's the balance —he was also never an isolationist. He shared companionship with his Hebrew brethren. In chapter 1, Daniel was listed as one among three other young Jewish men: Hananiah, Mishael, and Azariah. All four are named together as a tight-knit group of young men, bonded together by conviction and faith. In chapter 2, when the edict came to kill all the wise men of Babylon, including Daniel, we are told, "Daniel went to his house, and made the decision known to Hananiah, Mishael, and Azariah, his companions, that they might seek mercies from the God of heaven" (vv. 17–18). The word "companions" in this verse signifies that Daniel was in constant fellowship with them. When Daniel found out the problem, he announced, "Boys, we need to pray, and we need to pray *together*." Daniel was able to stand alone because he walked with others.

You and I will be able to stand alone for God only when we walk closely with others in fellowship. That's where we get the strength, the platform to do that. This is why we need fellowship. The Greek word for fellowship is *koinónia*. In the New Testament, *koinónia* has been translated *fellowship*, *partnership*, and *communion*. But it literally means "to share something with someone else." Fellowship is not just hanging out in Jesus' name. Sometimes church people manage to sanctify just about any activity we do simply by tagging the word "fellowship" on the end of it. So we have our weight lifters' fellowship, the left-handed basket-weaving fellowship, and so on. Just add "fellowship" to it and it's cool (with a hint of spirituality thrown in). But the biblical word means much more than just a social activity—more than getting together or being under the same roof on Sunday, and definitely more than just hanging out. Authentic biblical fellowship always has a spiritual component. Fellowship means I'm adding something good and godly to your life, and you're doing the same. It means we're mutually encouraging each other in spiritual matters, stimulating spiritual growth. And the reason for this is that we share a common love and devotion to Jesus Christ. We share Christ with one another! He is the glue that bonds our relationship together.

One author wrote, "Our churches are filled with people who outwardly look contented and at peace, but inwardly they are crying out for someone to love them just as they are."[4] People are crying out for *fellowship*, for authentic, mutually inspiring, and encouraging relationships in Christ. An old Jewish proverb says, "A friendless man is like a left hand bereft of the right hand." I might paraphrase it to say, "An isolated Christian is like a left hand with no right hand to go with it."

To begin with, an "isolated Christian" is an oxymoron. You can't have an isolated Christian—a Christian is part of the body of Christ. Proverbs 18:1 says, "A man who isolates himself seeks his own desire; he rages against all wise judgment." That's why as believers, we have a need to interact—a need for family.

Years ago, I came upon a little-known fact about Adolf Hitler. It turns out that Albert Speer, who was one of Hitler's closest associates, never really felt like his friend. Speer wrote, "Sometimes I asked myself: Why can't I call Hitler my friend? What is missing? I spent endless time with him, was almost at home in his private circle and, moreover, his foremost associate in his favorite field, architecture. Everything was missing. Never in my life have I met a person who so seldom revealed his feelings, and if he did so, instantly locked them away again."[5]

Daniel was able to stand alone and yet walk with others, connected to them. His life was in balance.

THE FUTURE IN THE PRESENT

A third area of Daniel's life that beautifully demonstrates balance is that though he saw into the future, he still lived in the present. One of the major features of the book of Daniel from chapter 7 all the way to chapter 12 is that it's mostly future-related, prophetic truth. God gave Daniel vision after vision of eschatological and apocalyptic truths. From Daniel's stand-point, all of it was "yet to come."

From Daniel's vantage point, he saw what was going on around him and what would come after him in terms of the Babylonian Empire, Medo-Persian Empire, the Grecian Empire, and the Roman Empire. After King Nebuchadnezzar saw in a dream a large image of gold, silver, bronze, iron, and iron mixed with clay, Daniel got the same information and revelation about four successive kingdoms, though he didn't see a statue. Instead he saw four rapacious beasts destroying each other and eating one another. Nebuchadnezzar saw history from the human viewpoint, but Daniel saw history from God's viewpoint. The human viewpoint is always impressive and shiny: "Look at the bling!" That's how we write our history. God sees the same thing, but He gives us the heart of it: human leaders can be like a bunch of animals trying to destroy each other.

You may recall the story of when Samuel was looking for the next king of Israel to follow Saul's reign. He went to the house of Jesse and he looked at Eliab, the oldest son. He was handsome and he *looked* like a king. But God said, "I have refused him. For the LORD does not see as man sees; for man looks at the outward appearance, but the LORD looks at the heart" (1 Samuel 16:7). It's the same with these visions in Daniel. Nebuchadnezzar saw the outward appearance of the kingdoms, but God showed Daniel the heart of the matter concerning the future. Daniel saw all of history, all the way to the coming of the Messiah and the setting up of His kingdom.

But even though Daniel saw into the future, he lived responsibly in his present world. That's a balancing act. He had one foot planted firmly in heaven and the other on earth. Some today believe it's unhealthy to teach prophecy. They say, "If you teach prophecy, it's distracting and unprofitable because you're getting people's minds off what is real and important now." I even heard of one pastor who boasted, "I never teach my people prophecy. I believe it's too distracting." A friend of his heard that and said, "Well, then you gotta admit, God sure has put a lot of distractions in the Bible."

Exactly! Because around one-fourth of the Bible is prophetic. It's as if God wrote it for us to be distracted a little bit about what's coming in the future. Let's consider four benefits of reading and understanding biblical prophecy.

PROPHECY IS MOTIVATING

First, prophecy is not distracting, but is rather incredibly *motivating*. When you study prophecy, it does something for you. It makes you confident in God because you realize that nothing takes God by surprise. He sees it all. He knows the future. He knew all about the future kings and kingdoms mentioned in Daniel because He is the one who wrote about it in detail and gave it to Daniel. So if God knows everything about coming history, then He must know about you and your future as well. Jesus said, "The very hairs of your head are all num-bered" (Matthew 10:30), meaning His intimate knowledge and concern for you is both specific and personal.

PROPHECY HELPS CLEAN UP YOUR LIFE

Another thing studying prophecy will do for you is to *clean up your life*. There is a close relationship between prophecy and godliness. When Peter predicted the end of the world and the coming of the end of the age, this is what he said: "Since all these things [around you] will be dissolved, what manner of persons ought you to be in holy conduct and godliness?" (2 Peter 3:11). When you see what is coming and that this world is going to be burned up, it changes the way you live. It makes you less of a materialistic person and more of a spiritual one. It will clean up your life.

PROPHECY COMFORTS YOU IN SORROW

A third benefit of prophecy is that it *comforts you in your sorrow*. All of us have loved ones, relatives, and friends who have died. They're no longer with us. But when we study prophecy, we learn not only about the coming Tribulation, but also about the coming King, His kingdom, future rewards, and a com-ing *reunion* with those who have died in Christ before us. That gives us comfort. And according to Paul, this prophetic truth is meant to be a massive dose of encouragement and comfort to all believers (1 Thessalonians 4:18).

PROPHECY CALLS YOU TO SERVICE

Fourth, *prophecy calls you to service.* It motivates you to serve the Lord, because you see in the future that you're going to stand before the judgment seat of Christ, and He will say to those who've been faithful, "Well done, good and faithful servant; you have been faithful over a few things, I will make you ruler over many things. Enter into the joy of your lord" (Matthew 25:23). That's motivating! I want to serve the Lord with all my heart, and there's nothing wrong with wanting Christ's commendation on that day.

So studying prophecy gives you a solid foundation in an unstable world. That's one reason that Daniel was so balanced. He was able to see into the future and use that information to live responsibly in the present. I agree with C. S. Lewis, who said, "The Christians who did most for the present world were just those who thought most of the next."[6]

BETTER WITH AGE

There's a fourth and final area of balance I want us to consider as we close out this book together. *Daniel aged gracefully, but he also influenced mightily.* Remember, when Daniel first came to Babylon he was only about fifteen or sixteen years of age. So he essentially grew up and grew old in Babylon. Eventually he also died and was buried in Babylon.

You would think a person who had been taken captive and transported to a foreign land to live there for so long would have had his soul crushed and his spirit broken. But not Daniel. Not only did he age in that foreign land, but he did so gracefully. The heart commitment he started with was maintained faithfully throughout his entire life. And as he grew in age, he also grew in influence. This guy made maximum impact. Every person who came in contact with Daniel—whether his contemporaries, his supervisors, or his king—was influenced by Daniel's integrity, his stand for God, and his work ethic. Even the king's wife described Daniel as "a man in your kingdom in whom is the Spirit of the Holy God" (Daniel 5:11).

I also believe Daniel influenced Cyrus, the Medo-Persian king, to let the Jews go back home after their seventy-year captivity. Daniel had been reading the writings of the prophet Jeremiah. He knew what the prophecy said, but I believe Daniel used his governmental influence to persuade Cyrus to sign the edict that allowed the Jews to go back home and rebuild Jerusalem.

And as we saw earlier, Daniel's influence reached far into the future, beyond his lifetime, all the way into the New Testament to the wise men from the East who came to Bethlehem. They said, "Where is He who has been born King of the Jews? For we have seen His star in the East and have come to worship Him" (Matthew 2:2). These were the Magi, who descended from the magicians in the court of Nebuchadnezzar. The Greek historian Herodotus referred to the Magi as a priestly caste of the Medes from Parthia and Mesopotamia who, after failing to overthrow the Persian Empire, became priestly advisers to the ancient Babylonian kings. In the court of Nebuchadnezzar, they were the highest-ranking officers of Babylon. These were the wise men of Babylon. And in chapter 2, Daniel was placed above all of the Magi in Babylon.

It's my conviction that since Daniel saw so far into the future, he saw the coming Jewish Messiah, wrote about Him, and then left all of that deposited work there in Babylon along with the Scripture scrolls that he had brought with him from Jerusalem. Isaiah the prophet had predicted that the people who walked in darkness would see a great light (Isaiah 9:2), and the Pentateuch promised "a Star" rising from Jacob that would point to a coming ruler (Numbers 24:17). We know for sure Daniel brought the book of Jeremiah with him. What Daniel saw in the Scriptures influenced those around him to the extent that years later, certain men would be captivated by a star in the heavens that led them to a Jewish Messiah in Bethlehem—a Messiah who one day will rule the world. That is *influence*. That is *balance*.

THREE AREAS TO BALANCE IN LIFE

I believe we as individual Christians and as a Christian community should live in balance like Daniel. We should know who we are and what we're about, and our lives should be lived in that harmonious place. At our church, Calvary Albuquerque, our mission statement is: "We pursue the God who is passionately pursuing a lost world." We do this by reaching *up*, reaching *in*, and reaching *out*. I believe these same areas were the areas of balance in Daniel's life.

REACHING UP

When we reach up, we express our adoration to God. This is our praying and our praising, our worshipping of God and our wondering over His majestic works, our music and our musings. We first connect upwardly in meaningful fellowship with God as the basis for being effective in our church and in our world.

REACHING IN

When we reach in, we explain the relevance of the Scriptures to our daily lives and build people up, fitting them for service in God's kingdom. After becoming connected with God we reach into the other parts of the body of Christ to strengthen fellow believers. In our church, we study together in a large assembly and then meet together in smaller groups to discuss the lessons we've learned and to pray for one another. We exercise our spiritual gifts for mutual edification.

REACHING OUT

When we reach out, we extend the love of God to a hurting world through evangelism and social concern. In his life, Daniel was all about these three critical areas: he reached *up*—worshipping God supremely. He reached *in*—tethered to a group of like-minded believers. And he reached *out*—influencing people who didn't know who God was.

Jules Léotard was a man who defied what most people thought was normal in the nineteenth century. Léotard was a man who dreamed of flying. In fact, he was so obsessed with the idea that he developed a whole new way humans could take to the air. He attached a bar to some cords suspended above his father's swimming pool, grabbed hold, and jumped. Then, while gliding through the air, he would let go of the swing . . . floating in midair until he caught another swing coming from the other side at just the right time, speed, velocity, and balance. He became the world's first trapeze artist. People were understandably astonished. A popular song was written about him during his 1860s heyday: "He'd fly through the air with the greatest of ease; a daring young man on the flying trapeze."[7] Léotard captured the public's fascination with his gravity-defying performances.

Like trapeze artists, you and I can also defy normal and walk on air—not just in dreams, but in *real life*. The Bible says, "The eternal God is your refuge, and underneath are the everlasting arms" (Deuteronomy 33:27). As followers of the one true God, we can fly to new heights because we are confident God's loving arms will be there to pick us up when we fall and one day carry us safely home.

Daniel the prophet was a man much like Jules Léotard. God gave him some big dreams. He didn't literally fly through the air, but he soared through amazingly trying circumstances with grace and ease. The odds seemed stacked against him. He was taken captive by the Babylonians and shuttled five hundred miles from his boyhood home. Throughout his life Daniel faced despair, discouragement, derision, and even death in this hostile foreign land. Yet he triumphed above his circumstances . . . even into old age. Daniel thrived in the midst of difficult situations that would have grounded most people in fear.

In chemistry, some gases are called inert because they don't react with any other substance. They just float around in the atmosphere. Other gases are highly reactive—they can combine with their surroundings and create anything from a new substance to an explosion, depending on what they're mixed with. People are meant to be reactive and interactive, not inert. Daniel could have remained inert—a stranger in a strange land—but instead he reacted with the people around him, influencing them and creating change in his community. He got down on his knees, and then he got in the mix. And even more astonishing, he left a legacy that continues to change people's lives today. Daniel's character and commitment set him head and shoulders above the rest.

I don't know what circumstances you are facing today, but I do know that with God's presence and help in your life, you, too, can rise above mediocrity and "just getting by." You're way too valuable to simply *exist* or be like everyone else in your generation. So lift your eyes above the crowd, above the horizon, and into the face of God. Gaze at the One who has already walked the road less traveled. And follow in His footsteps all the way home.

As the popular song goes, I urge you to "dare to be a Daniel, dare to stand alone! Dare to make God's purpose firm! Dare to make Him known!"[8]

You *can* defy normal!

DARE TO DEFY N⁰RMAL: BALANCE

One dictionary defines *balance* this way: "A condition in which different elements are equal or in the correct proportions."[9] That's a fitting word to describe the whole of Daniel's life— outwardly powerful yet inwardly stable. However, you can't have balance without the right perspective—God's. When it comes to God, the correct proportions may surprise you: He wants all of you. When you came to Christ, you gave Him your sinful life and He exchanged it for abundant, eternal life. In return, though, He wants complete owner's rights—you're under new management, after all. So the balanced life is not *a little of this, a little of that*—a little of the world and a little of God, a little selfishness and a little giving, a little apathy and a little concern. It's taking on God's view of your life and making it your own, letting His truth be the lens through which you see everything. My final dare to you is the most all-encompassing: I dare you to find true balance by becoming more fully God's in every way.

- *Deliberate*: How did Daniel worship God supremely and stay involved socially? Without engaging in the former, endeavoring in the latter is ultimately empty. If loving God is foremost in your life, every encounter—whether great or small—becomes an opportunity to glorify Him.

- *Defy Normal*: Create a core value statement for your life. Daniel "purposed in his heart" (Daniel 1:8) to love God first and foremost. That became the guiding principle in every decision and choice he made. What is your guiding principle, your core value statement? What is your commitment to God? Even if it's very similar to Daniel's, put it in your own words. Write it down, print it, and post it. If you want a real conversation starter, frame it. It will remind you of your purposeful choice, and at some point, you'll be asked about it.

- *Deliberate*: In what ways did Daniel stand alone yet still walk with others? To honor and obey God, Daniel often went against the flow, even if it meant no one stood with him. At the same time, he didn't let those experiences isolate him. He had mutual encouragement from like-minded friends. There are times when you will have to stand alone and other times when you'll need—and have—the support of friends; in both cases, know that God is with you.

- *Defy Normal*: Cultivate fellowship. "Let us consider one another in order to stir up love and good works, not forsaking the assembling of ourselves together, as is the manner of some, but exhorting one another, and so much the more as you see the Day [of the Lord] approaching" (Hebrews 10:24-25). Authentic Christian fellowship is more than just hanging out in Jesus' name; it's encouraging and stimulating like-minded brothers and sisters in biblical, God-glorifying ways. If you're not connected with other believers beyond church attendance, make connections. Join a small group or start your own. Trust God to redeem the time you invest in obeying His call to true fellowship.

- *Deliberate*: How did Daniel live in the present while also seeing the future? The story of Daniel's life alone is remarkable—flourishing in exile, thriving in the lions' den, serving several different kings in Babylon[10]—but his prophecy truly set him apart. He saw a God's-eye view of history, all the way up to Jesus' return and earthly kingdom. Daniel balanced such an incredible vision with an effective and responsible presence in his community by defying the norm.

- *Defy Normal*: Study biblical prophecy. Discover what God has told us about the future through His Word. Knowing prophecy will do four things for you:
  - ◻ Motivate you to trust God more completely
  - ◻ Helps you clean up your life and focus on living a more spiritual life
  - ◻ Comfort you with the thought of reunion with loved ones
  - ◻ Call you to serve God because you'll be rewarded accordingly

- *Deliberate*: How did Daniel age gracefully and continue to influence mightily? He came to Babylon as a teenager and lived his whole life there, growing old with grace. All along the way, he remained an effective influence for God. He kept his commitment to love God first throughout his long life, and God used him mightily, both during and after his life.
- *Defy Normal*: Commit to living in balance. Employ this threefold equilibrium that will help keep you balanced in your lifelong quest to defy normal:
  - ◻ Reach up. Express your adoration of God in praise and worship, with music and musings, every day.
  - ◻ Reach in. Look for the relevance of Scripture in your

everyday life. Connect first with God and then with other believers, first at church and then in small groups for encouragement, discussion, and prayer.

☐ Reach out. Make yourself available to God to help a hurting, lost world. Whether it's through evangelism, social justice, or serving your neighbors and coworkers in meaningful, heartfelt ways, be God's agent. You have good news—the best news—so let people know about it through your deeds and words.

NOTES

Note from an Unapologetic Nonconformist

1. Henry David Thoreau, "Economy," chap. 1 in *Walden* (1854; Iowa State University EServer, 2009), chap. 1, part A, 9, http://thoreau.eserver.org/walden1a.html.

2. *Merriam Webster Collegiate Online*, s.v. "status quo," accessed August 17, 2015, http://unabridged.merriam-webster.com/collegiate/status%20quo.

3. Karl Marx, "A Contribution to the Critique of Hegel's Philosophy of Right," *Deutsch-Französische Jahrbücher*, February 7 & 10, 1844, https://www.marxists.org/archive/marx/works/1843/critique-hpr/intro.htm.

Chapter 1: Conquer Your Inner Space: *Self-Control*

1. NASA, "July 20, 1969: One Giant Leap for Mankind," https://www.nasa.gov/mission_pages/apollo/apollo11.html.

2. Ibid.

3. M. R. DeHaan, *Bread for Each Day* (Grand Rapids: Zondervan, 1981), n.p.

4. AerospaceWeb, "Boeing 777 Long-Range Jetliner," http://www.aerospaceweb.org/aircraft/jetliner/b777.

5. Strabo, *Geography* XVI.1.5, trans. H. L. Jones, Loeb Classical Library ed. (1930; repr. Cambridge, MA: Harvard University Press, 1961).

6. Brittany Garcia, "Ishtar Gate," in *Ancient History Encyclopedia*, article published August 23, 2013, http://www.ancient.eu/Ishtar_Gate.

7. John F. Walvoord, "Early Life of Daniel in Babylon," chap. 1 in *Daniel: The Key to Prophetic Revelation*, August 12, 2007, http://www.walvoord.com/article/242.

Chapter 2: Risk or No Reward: *Faith*

1. *Step into Liquid*, written and directed by Dana Brown (2003; Santa Monica, CA: Artisan Entertainment, 2004), DVD.

2. Adapted from John Bisagno, quoted in John Maxwell, *Today Matters* (Nashville: Center Street, 2004), 205.

3. William Shakespeare, *History of Henry IV*, Part II, act 3, scene 1.

4. Warren W. Wiersbe, *The Bible Exposition Commentary*, vol. 1 (Colorado Springs: Victor, 2003), 594–95.

5. The British Museum, "Nebuchadnezzar II, King of Babylon (605–562 BC)," The British Museum, accessed August 20, 2015, http://www.britishmuseum.org/explore/highlights/article_index/n/nebuchadnezzar_ii.aspx.

6. Johanna Tudeau, "Nabu (god)," *Ancient Mesopotamian Gods and Goddesses*, Oracc and the UK Higher Education Academy, http://oracc.museum.upenn.edu/amgg/listofdeities/nabu.

7. Sarah Jio, "9 Things You Didn't Know about Dreams," WebMD feature from *Woman's Day*, November 1, 2012, http://www.webmd.com/balance/features/9-things-about-dreams.

8. "Creative Proverbs from Denmark," Creative Proverbs from Around the World, accessed August 20, 2015, http://creativeproverbs.com/da01.htm.

9. Corrie ten Boom, *Tramp for the Lord* (Fort Washington, PA: CLC Publications, 1974), 12.

10. Larry Shannon-Misal, "Americans' Belief in God, Miracles and Heaven Decline," *The Harris Poll* #97, December 16, 2013, http://www.harrisinteractive.com/NewsRoom /HarrisPolls/tabid/447/ctl/ReadCustom%20Default/mid/1508/ArticleId/1353 /Default.aspx.

11. Luis Lugo, "The Decline of Institutional Religion," (presented at Faith Angle Forum, South Beach, Florida, March 18, 2013), http://www.washingtonpost.com/r/2010-2019 /WashingtonPost/2013/03/25/Editorial-Opinion/Graphics/Pew-Decline-of -Institutional-Religion.pdf.

12. Elizabeth Cheney, "Overheard in an Orchard," quoted in Alonzo Bernard Webber, *Stories and Poems for Public Addresses* (Charleston, SC: Nabu Press, 2011).

13. G. Stringer Rowe, *James Calvert of Fiji* (London: Charles H. Kelly, 1893), http://archive .org/stream/jamescalvertoffi00roweiala/jamescalvertoffi00roweiala_djvu.txt.

14. John Chase, "Graduates Skirt Prayer Ban," *Chicago Tribune*, May 21, 2001, http://articles.chicagotribune.com/2001-05-21/news/0105210103_1_silent-prayer -invocation-and-benediction-graduating.

Chapter 3: Go Low: *Humility*

1. John P. Eaton and Charles A. Haas, *Titanic: Triumph and Tragedy* (New York: W. W. Norton, 1994), 115.

2. Joseph Parker, quoted in W. R. Moody, ed., *Record of Christian Work*, vol. 18 (New York: Fleming H. Revell, 1899), 111.

3. William Ernest Henley, "Invictus," in Louis Untermeyer, ed., *Modern British Poetry* (New York: Harcourt, Brace and Howe, 1920), #, http://www.bartleby.com/103/7.html.

4. Jan van der Crabben, "Cyrus II," in *Ancient History Encyclopedia*, article published April 28, 2011, http://www.ancient.eu/Cyrus_II.

5. "Me, Me, Me! America's `Narcissism Epidemic,'" excerpted from Jean M. Twenge and W. Keith Campbell, *The Narcissism Epidemic* (New York: Simon and Schuster, 2009), *Today* Pop Culture, April 20, 2009, http://www.today.com/popculture/me-me-me -americas-narcissism-epidemic-2D80555351.

6. Jim Taylor, "Narcissism is Alive and Well in America," *The Power of Prime* (blog), *Psychology Today*, May 16, 2011, https://www.psychologytoday.com/blog/the-power -prime/201105/narcissism-is-alive-and-well-in-america.

Chapter 4: Find a Hill Worth Dying On: *Integrity*

1. Oscar Hammerstein II, *Lyrics* (Milwaukee, WI: Hal Leonard Books, 1985), 45–46.

2. Oswald Chambers, quoted in Martin H. Manser, comp., *The Westminster Collection of Christian Quotations* (Louisville, KY: Westminster John Knox Press, 2001), 191.

3. Historians struggle to clarify the ancestral history of Mede and Persian rulers. The ancient Greek historian Xenophon named "Gubaru" (also translated Gobryas) in his

Cyropaedia as the governor of Persian Babylon. Various theories try to identify Darius the Mede beyond the book of Daniel. William Shea offers evidence of a coregency in which Darius (under his family name Cambyses) and Cyrus shared rule over Babylon. See William H. Shea, "Darius the Mede: An Update," *Andrews University Seminary Studies*, 20, no. 3 (Autumn 1982): 229–247, http://www.auss.info/auss_publication_file.php?pub_id=654. Shea also weighs in on the likelihood of Gubaru and Darius being one and the same. In Josef Karst's translation of the early church father Eusebius, he found evidence that a king named Darius existed at the same time as Cyrus the Great and had at least partial control of newly conquered Babylon. See Josef Karst, ed., *Die Chronik aus dem Armenischen übersetzt mit textkritischem Commentar.* Vol. 5 of *Eusebius Werke. Die griechischen christlichen Schriftseller der ersten drei Jahrhunderte*, vol. 20 (Leipzig: J. C. Hinrichs, 1911), 246.

4.   William Carey, as quoted in Kay Arthur, *Lord, I Need Grace to Make It Today* (Colorado Springs: WaterBrook, 2000), 186–87.

5.   "Thomas Edison," Biography.com, accessed August 23, 2015, http://www.biography.com /people/thomas-edison-9284349.

6.   "Frank Lloyd Wright," Biography.com, accessed August 23, 2015, http://www.biography .com/people/frank-lloyd-wright-9537511.

7.   Jack Zavada, "John Wesley Biography," About.com, About Religion & Spirituality, accessed August 23, 2015, http://christianity.about.com/od/methodistdenomination/a /John-Wesley.htm.

8.   Eugene H. Peterson, *A Long Obedience in the Same Direction* (Downers Grove, IL: InterVarsity, 2000).

9.   "Lord Acton Quote Archive," Acton Institute for the Study of Religion and Liberty, accessed August 23, 2015, http://www.acton.org/research/lord-acton-quote-archive.

10.   "Billy Graham Makes Most Admired Men List," CBN News, January 1, 2014, http://www .cbn.com/cbnnews/us/2013/December/Billy-Graham-Makes-Most-Admired-Men-List.

11.   "Boldt Action," Snopes.com, last updated March 11, 2007, http://www.snopes.com/glurge /waldorf.asp.

12.   Jim Elliot, quoted in Elisabeth Elliot, *Through Gates of Splendor* (Carol Stream, IL: Tyndale, 2015), 20; emphasis in original.

13.   William Barclay, *The New Daily Study Bible: The Gospel of John,* vol. 1 (Louisville, KY: Westminster John Knox Press, 2001), 204.

14.   "Persecution in the Early Church," ReligionFacts, accessed August 23, 2015, http://www .religionfacts.com/christianity/history/persecution; Sophie Lunn-Rockliffe, "Christianity and the Roman Empire," BBB, last updated February 17, 2011, http://www.bbc.co.uk /history/ancient/romans/christianityromanempire_article_01.shtml.

15.   Tracy Connor, "NYC Cabbie Gets Life for Pakistan 'Honor Killings,'" NBC News, May 8, 2015, http://www.nbcnews.com/news/us-news/pakistan-honor-killing-sentence-n355481; Daniel Akbari and Paul Tereault, *Honor Killing* (Bloomington, IN: AuthorHouse, 2014), 229.

16.   John Foxe, "The Beginnings of General Persecutions Against the Church (AD 54–304)," chap. 2 in *Foxe's Book of Martyrs* (Grand Rapids: Baker, 1999).

17.   George H. Edeal, "Why the Choir Was Late," *Life Magazine,* March 27, 1950, 19–23.

18. Adapted from Peter Marshall, quoted in Charles R. Swindoll, "The Keeper of the Spring," *Improving Your Serve: The Art of Unselfish Living* (Nashville: Thomas Nelson, 1981) #.

Chapter 5: Rise Above: *Dependence*

1. Franklin Graham, "Politics of Prayer," *Washington Times*, January 19, 2009, http://www .washingtontimes.com/news/2009/jan/19/politics-of-prayer.

2. Dan Gilgoff, "A New Tradition for Obama's Presidential Events: Opening with a Prayer," *U.S. News & World Report*, February 24, 2009, http://www.usnews.com/news/blogs/god -and-country/2009/02/24/a-new-tradition-for-obamas-presidential-events-opening-with -a-prayer.

3. Cheryl K. Chumley, "Atheist Group Blames School for Student Reciting the Lord's Prayer at Graduation," *Washington Times*, June 7, 2013, http://www.washingtontimes .com/news/2013/jun/7/atheist-group-blames-school-student-reciting-lords/.

4. Charles Haddon Spurgeon, quoted in "80 Charles Spurgeon Quotes on Prayer," no. 76, *Prayer Coach*, October 4, 2010, http://prayer-coach.com/2010/10/04/prayer-quotes -charles-spurgeon/.

5. R. A. Torrey, *Rewards of Prayer* , chap. 4 (New Kensington, PA: Whitaker House, 2002).

6. D. L. Moody, quoted in J. Wilbur Chapman, "Introductory," chap. 1 in *The Life and Work of Dwight Lyman Moody (Philadelphia, Gillespie & Metzgar, 1900)*, http://www .revival-library.org/catalogues/1882ff/chapman.html.

7. Leonard Ravenhill, "Heart Breathings, Excerpt 19" part 4, http://www.ravenhill.org /heartb19.htm.

8. *International Directory of Company Histories*, vol. 17 (St. James, MO: St. James Press, 1997), quoted in "TCBY Enterprises Inc. History," Funding Universe, http://www .fundinguniverse.com/company-histories/tcby-enterprises-inc-history.

9. *Amen* means "so be it" or "do it."

Chapter 6: Get on Your Knees and Fight: *Courage*

1. Frank Newport, "Americans More Likely to Believe in God Than the Devil, Heaven More Than Hell," Gallup News Service, June 13, 2007, http://www.gallup.com/poll /27877/americans-more-likely-believe-god-than-devil-heaven-more-than-hell.aspx.

2. C. S. Lewis, *The Screwtape Letters* (New York: Simon & Schuster, 1996), ix.

3. John White, *The Fight* (Downers Grove, IL: InterVarsity, 1976), 16.

4. William Cowper, "Exhortation to Prayer," in *Poems,* vol. 2 (Boston: E. Lincoln, 1802), XXVIII.

5. Martin Luther, as quoted in J. Oswald Sanders, *Spiritual Leadership* (Chicago: Moody, 1974), 76.

Chapter 7: Look Out and Look Up: *Hope*

1. George Santayana, *The Life of Reason,* vol. 1, *Reason in Common Sense* (New York: C. Scribner's Sons, 1905)(Amherst, NY: Prometheus Books, 1998), 82.

2. John Bagot Glubb, *The Fate of Empires* (Edinburgh, Scotland: William Blackwood & Sons, 1977), 24.

3. Josephus, *The War of the Jews*, book 6, chapter 9, from *The Works of Josephus*, trans. William Whiston (Peabody, MA: Hendrickson, 1987).

4. Charles Matson Odahl, *Constantine and the Christian Empire* (New York: Routledge, 2010), 250.

5. Felix Halpern, *Restoring the Ancient Paths* (Maitland, FL: Xulon, 2010), 133.

6. Berel Wein, adapted by Yaakov Astor, "The Black Death," JewishHistory.org, http://www.jewishhistory.org/the-black-death.

7. "Spain Passes Citizenship Plan for Descendants of Jews Exiled Centuries Ago," BBC News, June 11, 2015, http://www.bbc.com/news/world-europe-33102891.

8. Winston Churchill, quoted in Paul Eidelberg, *A Jewish History of Philosophy* (Bloomington, IN: iUniverse, 2004), 121.

9. Henry Ward Beecher, quoted in Edward L. Harris, *The Quest* (Maitland, FL: Xulon, 2010), 142.

10. Corrie ten Boom, quoted in Roy B. Zuck, *The Speaker's Quote Book* (Grand Rapids: Kregel, 2009), 526.

11. Roberta Lee, *The SuperStress Solution: 4-Week Diet and Lifestyle Program* (New York: Random House, 2010), chap. 8.

12. Rich Deem, "Scientific Studies That Show a Positive Effect of Religion on Health," Evidence for God, http://www.godandscience.org/apologetics/religionhealth.html. Deem cites an extensive list of studies in support of the claim that religion, faith, and spirituality have a positive effect on the recovery of the ill and injured. In particular, see J. L. Florell, *Bulletin of the American Protestant Hospital Association* 37, no. 2 (1973): 29–36.

13. Yang Jisheng, "China's Great Shame," *New York Times,* November 13, 2012, http://www.nytimes.com/2012/11/14/opinion/chinas-great-shame.html.

14. "Cambodia's Brutal Khmer Rouge Regime," BBC News, August 4, 2014, http://www.bbc.com/news/world-asia-pacific-10684399.

15. "World War II History," History.com, 2009, accessed August 23, 2015, http://www.history.com/topics/world-war-ii/world-war-ii-history.

16. "Plague: History," Centers for Disease Control and Prevention, last updated November 18, 2014, http://www.cdc.gov/plague/history.

17. "Black Death," History.com, 2010, accessed August 23, 2015, http://www.history.com/topics/black-death.

18. D. Martyn Lloyd-Jones, *Spiritual Depression: Its Causes and Its Cure* (Grand Rapids: Eerdmans, 1965), 20.

Chapter 8: Reach Up, In, and Out: *Balance*

1. "Smoker Plunges 65 Feet," *Daily Record and Sunday Mail*, July 18, 2001, quoted in Humorlist, July 19, 2001, http://archive.thehumorlist.us/Site1/Digests/H0107190.php.

2. W. A. Criswell, "Do or Die Decisions," W. A. Criswell Sermon Library, May 3. 1970,

http://www.wacriswell.com/sermons/1970/do-or-die-decision.

3. John Wesley, quoted in David Lyle Jeffrey, ed., *English Spirituality in the Age of Wesley* (Vancouver, BC: Regent College Publishing, 2000), 247.

4. Keith Miller, *The Taste of New Wine*, quoted in Howard Snyder, *The Problem of Wineskins* (Downers Grove, IL: InterVarsity, 1975), 90.

5. Albert Speer, *Inside the Third Reich* (New York: Simon and Schuster, 1970), 100.

6. C. S. Lewis, *Mere Christianity* (New York: HarperCollins, 1952), chap. 10.

7. "Jules Léotard," Victoria and Albert Museum, accessed August 23, 2015, http://www.vam.ac.uk/content/articles/j/jules-leotard.

8. Philip P. Bliss, "Dare to Be a Daniel," lyrics, 1873.

9. *Oxford English Dictionary*, s.v. "balance," http://www.oxforddictionaries.com/us/definition/american_english/balance.

10. The Bible mentions Daniel's service under four rulers: Nebuchadnezzar (604–569 BC; see Daniel 2:48–49), Belshazzar (the regent of Nabonidus in 539 BC; see Daniel 5:29–31), Darius the Mede (probably Gubaru, regent for Cyrus beginning in 539 BC; see Daniel 6:1–2), and Cyrus of Persia (see Daniel 6:28). History records the names of other kings of Babylon whom Daniel would have also served: Amel-marduk (561–560 BC; also known as Evil-Merodach of 2 Kings 25:27 and Jeremiah 52:31), Nergal-shar-usur (559–556 BC; also known as Neriglissar and Nergal-Sharezer of Jeremiah 39:3), Labashi-marduk (556 BC; also known as Labosoarchad), and Nabonidus (555–539 BC; also known as Nabu-na'id). See H. W. F. Saggs, *The Babylonians* (London: The Folio Society, 1999), 119–24.

ABOUT THE AUTHOR

Called "one of the best Bible teachers in the country" by Franklin Graham, Skip Heitzig served under Chuck Smith at Calvary Chapel of Costa Mesa until 1981. He went on to found Calvary Albuquerque, which today ministers to more than fifteen thousand people.

Skip has authored over two dozen books, including *The Daily God Book, You Can Understand the Book of Revelation,* and *How to Study the Bible and Enjoy It.* Skip and Lenya have been married for over thirty years and currently live in Albuquerque, New Mexico.

IF YOU ENJOYED THIS BOOK, WILL YOU CONSIDER SHARING THE MESSAGE WITH OTHERS?

Mention the book in a blog post or through Facebook, Twitter, Pinterest, or upload a picture through Instagram.

Recommend this book to those in your small group, book club, workplace, and classes.

Head over to facebook.com/worthypublishing, "LIKE" the page, and post a comment as to what you enjoyed the most.

Tweet "I recommend reading #DefyingNormal by @SkipHeitzig // @worthypub"

Pick up a copy for someone you know who would be challenged and encouraged by this message.

Write a book review online.

Visit us at worthypublishing.com

twitter.com/worthypub

worthypub.tumblr.com

facebook.com/worthypublishing

pinterest.com/worthypub

instagram.com/worthypub

youtube.com/worthypublishing

Steps to Peace With God

1. God's Purpose: Peace and Life

God loves you and wants you to experience peace and life—abundant and eternal.

The Bible Says ...

"We have peace with God through our Lord Jesus Christ." *Romans 5:1, NKJV*

"For God so loved the world that He gave His only begotten Son, that whoever believes in Him should not perish but have everlasting life." *John 3:16, NKJV*

"I have come that they may have life, and that they may have it more abundantly." *John 10:10, NKJV*

Since God planned for us to have peace and the abundant life right now, why are most people not having this experience?

2. Our Problem: Separation From God

God created us in His own image to have an abundant life. He did not make us as robots to automatically love and obey Him, but gave us a will and a freedom of choice.

We chose to disobey God and go our own willful way. We still make this choice today. This results in separation from God.

The Bible Says ...

"For all have sinned and fall short of the glory of God." *Romans 3:23, NKJV*

"For the wages of sin is death, but the gift of God is eternal life in Christ Jesus our Lord." *Romans 6:23, NKJV*

Our choice results in separation from God.

People (Sinful)

God (Holy)

Our Attempts

Through the ages, individuals have tried in many ways to bridge this gap ... without success ...

The Bible Says ...

"There is a way that seems right to a man, but its end is the way of death."
Proverbs 14:12, NKJV

"But your iniquities have separated you from your God; and your sins have hidden His face from you, so that He will not hear."
Isaiah 59:2, NKJV

There is only one remedy for this problem of separation.

3. God's Remedy: The Cross

Jesus Christ is the only answer to this problem. He died on the cross and rose from the grave, paying the penalty for our sin and bridging the gap between God and people.

The Bible Says ...

"For there is one God and one Mediator between God and men, the Man Christ Jesus."
1 Timothy 2:5, NKJV

"For Christ also suffered once for sins, the just for the unjust, that He might bring us to God."
1 Peter 3:18, NKJV

"But God shows his love for us in that while we were still sinners, Christ died for us." *Romans 5:8, ESV*

God has provided the only way ... we must make the choice ...

4. OUR RESPONSE: RECEIVE CHRIST

We must trust Jesus Christ and receive Him by personal invitation.

THE BIBLE SAYS ...

"Behold, I stand at the door and knock. If anyone hears My voice and opens the door, I will come in to him and dine with him, and he with Me." *Revelation 3:20, NKJV*

"But to all who did receive him, who believed in his name, he gave the right to become children of God." *John 1:12, ESV*

"If you confess with your mouth that Jesus is Lord and believe in your heart that God raised him from the dead, you will be saved." *Romans 10:9, ESV*

Are you here ... or here?

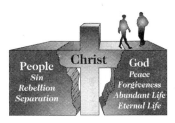

Is there any good reason why you cannot receive Jesus Christ right now?

HOW TO RECEIVE CHRIST:

1. Admit your need (say, "I am a sinner").
2. Be willing to turn from your sins (repent) and ask for God's forgiveness.
3. Believe that Jesus Christ died for you on the cross and rose from the grave.
4. Through prayer, invite Jesus Christ to come in and control your life through the Holy Spirit (receive Jesus as Lord and Savior).

WHAT TO PRAY:

Dear God,
 I know that I am a sinner. I want to turn from my sins, and I ask for Your forgiveness. I believe that Jesus Christ is Your Son. I believe He died for my sins and that You raised Him to life. I want Him to come into my heart and to take control of my life. I want to trust Jesus as my Savior and follow Him as my Lord from this day forward.

In Jesus' Name, amen.

_____   _____
Date   Signature

God's Assurance: His Word

If You Prayed This Prayer,

The Bible Says ...

"For 'everyone who calls on the name of the Lord will be saved.'"
Romans 10:13, ESV

Did you sincerely ask Jesus Christ to come into your life? Where is He right now? What has He given you?

"For by grace you have been saved through faith. And this is not your own doing; it is the gift of God, not a result of works, so that no one may boast." *Ephesians 2:8–9, ESV*

The Bible Says ...

"He who has the Son has life; he who does not have the Son of God does not have life. These things I have written to you who believe in the name of the Son of God, that you may know that you have eternal life, and that you may continue to believe in the name of the Son of God." *1 John 5:12–13, NKJV*

Receiving Christ, we are born into God's family through the supernatural work of the Holy Spirit, who indwells every believer. This is called regeneration or the "new birth."

This is just the beginning of a wonderful new life in Christ. To deepen this relationship you should:

1. Read your Bible every day to know Christ better.
2. Talk to God in prayer every day.
3. Tell others about Christ.
4. Worship, fellowship, and serve with other Christians in a church where Christ is preached.
5. As Christ's representative in a needy world, demonstrate your new life by your love and concern for others.

God bless you as you do.

Franklin Graham

If you want further help in the decision you have made, write to:
Billy Graham Evangelistic Association
1 Billy Graham Parkway, Charlotte, NC 28201-0001

1-877-2GRAHAM (1-877-247-2426)
BillyGraham.org/commitment